"Unravel the Real Truth About Goal Setting!"

THE ULTIMATE CHEATSHEET ON GOAL SETTING

KUNAL SACHDEVA

PRABHAT PAPERBACKS

Publisher
PRABHAT PAPERBACKS
4/19 Asaf Ali Road, New Delhi–110 002
Ph. 23289555 • 23289666 • 23289777 • Helpline/ 7827007777
e-mail: prabhatbooks@gmail.com • Website: www.prabhatbooks.com

Edition
First, 2022

Price
Three Hundred Rupees only

ISBN 978-93-5521-059-3

Printed at
Sanjay Printer, Sahibabad

THE ULTIMATE CHEATSHEET ON GOAL SETTING
by Kunal Sachdeva

ISBN 978-93-5521-059-3

₹ 300.00

I dedicate this to my mother **Dr. Neera Sachdeva,**
whom I have always admired as an example of courage, hard work and perseverance.
It is her optimism and belief that has always encouraged me to go ahead be what may be.
Without her patience, understanding, support and most above all love, the completion of this work would not have been possible.

Preface

Why another goal-setting book?

Because the majority of people want to be successful, but at the same time they do not know what to do about it and how to get the best out of their life. They let their days pass by in mediocrity without even realizing the possibility of a happy and fulfilling life.

You cannot achieve anything till you aim for it. How do you expect to be successful in your endeavors till you know what to achieve?

The best way to realize and tap the potential and power a day holds in your life is through the power of goal setting.

Instead of you living your life in circles, the methods in this book will help you set your goals aligned to your core values and will help you create a roadmap to success for yourself. The techniques in this book will guide you to live a meaningful life based solely on your choices, your beliefs, and your aspirations. Be it searching for something that you have always valued like peace or love, or something tangible like a luxury house or a car, this book will provide you the tools to set goals and achieve them.

This book will teach you the methods of setting meaningful

goals and living a purposeful life, rather than spending your days, months, and years in confusion and mediocrity.

The best way to read this book is to either read it section-wise or to treat every question as an independent one. Each section when read separately will give the reader a clear idea of the concept the chapter explains. Each question when read independently is also enough to get you the answer you need.

Wish you a happy reading.

❑

Acknowledgements

I would like to express my gratitude to my loved ones who saw me through this book; to all those who provided support, talked things over, read, wrote, offered comments, allowed me to quote their remarks and assisted in the editing, proofreading and design.

A special thank you to my partner, **Sharad Gujar** for his strength and support in getting all our projects to life. Nobody has been more important to me in this journey than my team. I would like to specially thank **Suraj Harpude, Prashant Ramchandani, Saurabh Rawat, Kishor Shelar** and **Jaiprakash Singh** who have been the strongest pillars in my journey. I would also like to acknowledge **Jeetendra Singh** and **Rishi Jha** for rendering their unending support.

Also I would like to thank **Amit Bajaj**, for being my mentor and encouraging me to write this book.

Always a part of my journey as a guiding star, I would like to thank my ideal Late **Mr R. Varman**, who taught me the basics of Art Direction, **Ashish Ranade**, for being my mentor and guide me during my learning days and **Malay Dey**, my drawing teacher in school, who taught me how to achieve my first goal.

Nobody has been more important to me in the pursuit of this project than the members of my family. I would like to thank my parents **Dr. Ashok Sachdeva** and **Seema Sachdeva**, whose love and guidance are with me in whatever I pursue. They are the ultimate role models.

Also a very special thank you to my brother **Sampark Sachdeva**, for making me to commit to write this book.

Most importantly, I wish to thank my loving and supportive wife, **Romi Sachdeva**, who provided unending inspiration to get my ideas on paper.

Last and not least: "I beg forgiveness of all those who have been with me over the course of the years and whose names I have failed to mention."

❑

Meet Kunal Sachdeva

Kunal Sachdeva is an expert in Art Direction and Set Designing whose accomplishments include:

Education:

- Bachelor of Fine Arts (B.F.A.) Applied Arts

Work History:

- Art Director, 2009 to 2019
- Co-Founder, **Vertex** - 2011
- Co-Founder, **Vertex Transport** - 2018
- Production Designer 2020 to date
- Co-Founder, **V Flex** - 2020

Personal Info:

Kunal Sachdeva is a well-known name in the Bollywood fraternity, not only as one of the leading Production Designers & Art Director, but also as a serial entrepreneur.

He started out over two decades ago, as an assistant art

director and over the years has gone up the ranks transforming the look of over 100 Bollywood films & TV shows.

Kunal's first taste of entrepreneurship was in 2008 when he along with his close friend, and now business partner, **Sharad Gujar**, invested a mere Rs. 30,000 in buying & renting a few handheld machines.

2011 was the breakaway year where Kunal and Sharad co-founded **Vertex**, an Art Direction company, which over the last decade has grown to be one of the top prop design companies in Bollywood.

This was followed by 2 more successful ventures - **Vertex Transport** in 2018 and **V Flex** (Printing & Design) in 2020.

Today the three combined have a turnover into crores and serve almost all of the top Bollywood film and television production houses.

Kunal has been a true leader, standing by his team at all times both professionally & personally. He goes by the belief, that it's the people who make the business & not the other way around.

In addition to this, he loves binging on documentaries, books & old hindi songs.

Through this book, Kunal has shared the various goal setting methods that he has learnt and used, which have been the foundation of all the success he has gone onto achieve.

❑

Contents

Chapter 1

Visualization

"Visualize what you want to do before you do it. Visualization is so powerful that when you know what you want, you will get it."
–Audrey Flack

1. The potter's little piece of wisdom

Let us use our imagination and create a picture in our mind as we read this story about a young social worker named Tarun and an old potter named Manya. Every morning while walking towards his office in the nearby village, Tarun would cross Manya's house. He would often see Manya sitting in his open verandah at the potter's wheel, with his hands covered with clay, creating one of his beautiful pots. Often Tarun would not pay much attention towards Manya, and while being engrossed in his own thoughts would quietly pass by Manya's house.

Soon it was Diwali season and it was time for everyone to decorate their houses with lamps, lights and flowers. That evening, Tarun's wife requested him to buy a few *diyas* to light up around the house. Tarun promised her that he will get a few while on his way back from his office the next day.

The next evening, he decided to stop at Manya's house and pick a few diyas that his wife wanted. Manya's house had an open verandah with a room to one side of it. A mud compound wall ran across the small house, which had a few shelves made in it. As Tarun stepped into the verandah, he saw no one around. Pots and vessels, were lined up everywhere. Strangely, he had never noticed them in detail, whenever he passed Manya's place on his way to his office. A few shelves on the sides had beautiful pottery, while the potter's wheel with molded clay occupied the little open space in the middle. "Perhaps the potter is not at home," Tarun thought.

Suddenly, a very beautiful, small sized, earthen pot caught his eye. He could not help admiring the intricate design that had been carefully carved around the borders of the pot. Few floral motifs ran around the middle, while a patterned border ran around the lower circumference. He touched the pot and felt the delicate carvings.

He slowly picked it up and felt its weight in his hand. It was heavy, but the detailed design made it look very delicate and tender. He ran his hands around the design and gently put it back on the shelf.

As he moved his gaze from that pot to the nearby shelf, he got carried away with the beauty of the other pots as well. Varied in size and design, each one was as beautiful as the other. Tarun was awestruck by the amount of detail each of them had. Few with floral carvings, others with ethnic patterns, every one of them had their own unique design. Manya was no less than an artist, he thought.

As Tarun looked ahead, he noticed that the door of Manya's room was half open. He slowly moved towards it, being careful not to step on the bags of clay, and a few pots scattered around. As he reached the door, Tarun gently opened it and peeked inside.

It was a small room with just a window on the side to illuminate the surroundings. Right in the middle of the room was Manya seated cross-legged on a *dari*, with his eyes closed. He had a very calm expression on his face, almost as if in a meditative state. As Tarun stepped in, Manya gently opened his eyes saw Tarun at the door and gave him a warm smile.

Tarun got a little conscious, gave Manya a curious look and, asked him. "What are you doing?"

Manya replied back, "Nothing much son. I'm just sitting and thinking of a new design for my pots."

"But isn't this a stranger way to imagine," said Tarun. "You could have done it while working on your pots? You are actually sitting and doing nothing."

"No, son, it's not what you think." Manya replied in a calm voice. "You must have noticed the various designs on the pots that are kept outside. Apart from making regular, pots and vessels, I spend some time with myself, creating unique designs and patterns for myself. It helps me improve upon my skill, and at the same time these pots get me a far better price in the market due to their uniqueness."

"I also make sure that I keep working towards improving upon my patterns so that my designs don't become boring and repetitive," continued Manya. "What I was doing here was to trying to imagine each and every detail of the next pot I will create."

"Even before I touch the pottery wheel, I try creating the image of the pot I will make in a very vivid and clear manner. When I do this, I don't see any obstacles or problems, I just see the finished pot in my hands. Then when I sit down to work, my purpose is just to turn the creation of my mind into a reality. My work is very special to me, and doing this exercise every day, helps me to bring immense improvement in my creations." Then Manya gave Tarun a warm smile and asked his purpose of coming to his house.

Later, Tarun went home with his diyas. He also bought the small pot that he had picked up from the shelf. He just could not leave it behind because of its beauty.

Can you not admire the wisdom of the old potter? Here is a man who totally understands the power of his imagination. His method of keeping time aside to concentrate and paint picture of his works in his mind is commendable. Here Manya does not worry about how he will get things together, or how he will sell his pots, he simply imagines a complete pot in his mind and sets off to create it in its physical form. This is the kind of devotion that we must cultivate to turn our dreams into reality. Just as Manya did, we must use the power of our imagination to create in our minds, whatever we want to manifest in our reality. Our subconscious mind, then follows these instructions to help us take action, in order to achieve what we created in our mind. This is what visualization is all about.

Here is a wise old potter, who has a definite purpose and who knows how to improve upon his creations. His power of visualization helps him create more and more beautiful, pots and gives him immense satisfaction at the same time.

Having a purpose and visualizing it is very important for every person. It keeps you aligned with your passion, and with your goals. This leads us to move on the correct path, do our duties correctly and to enrich our souls. It is these actions that define our destiny.

For Tarun, it was not about just getting the diyas anymore. What an old potter had taught him, was something he would never forget. It was time for him to search for a purpose in life, and to use his imagination to create it in his physical world.

2. Seeing what lies ahead

Have you ever imagined what your dream life would be like?

Imagine you are leading a life with a successful career. You already have a well-paid and satisfying job, which also spares you the time to spend with your family and friends.

Now please sit and ponder upon the thought… Would you be able to identify the steps needed for you to live this ideal life of yours?

You might be able to identify them clearly, but the struggle lies in between where you are and where you would like to be.

It is relatively easy to imagine the end. It's quite simple to see how everything you have imagined will fit perfectly in the end. But the struggle for everything comes in getting from point A to point B...

We often think that by doing mere hard work we can get the results we desire. But here lies the problem. Just the willingness to do hard work won't let you identify the opportunities that come by your way.

Mostly opportunities are not easy to spot, if you yourself are not clear with what you are looking for. This is where visualization comes in.

There might be times when you might not know what you truly want... In those times your visualization focusses on the wrong thing.

But even if you get that right, then also things might not be very easy for you. You will still have to recognize opportunities as and when they come.

This is the time to utilize the power of visualization fully.

Visualization helps train your mind so that you begin to spot the opportunities in life. The more often you repeat the process of visualizing your goals, the better your mind gets with identifying them.

But only visualizing will not get you near your desired goal.

You still have to take action.

The difficult part is when you abandon all excuses, fears and distractions and get going after getting the most out of that opportunity.

It might be difficult in the beginning and one may get distracted very easily. Since change is always hard to accept and act upon, this makes it difficult for the process of execution to set in.

At times you might even think that you don't deserve this.

Don't let this feeling stop you from achieving what you desired for.

This is where you have to commit and not quit.

Visualization will not work till you know how to use it to your advantage. It's you who has to take charge of your life. Instead of sitting and merely visualizing your target, and imagining for things to happen on their own, it is better to do it the right way.

Sharpening and focusing the mind should be something that needs to be done on a daily basis. Visualization isn't a shortcut to better things. It will not work on its own. It takes belief. It takes action.

3. Answer these 'Right now' questions...

A very important part of goal setting is to realign your vision by introspecting and pondering upon where you need to get to. Most people never do that. Realistically speaking, only 8% of people manage to achieve their goals in life. The reason why they get stuck is because they never think about or are never told about what they need to do to get what they want in life.

Setting a goal for your life should be like writing a script on yourself. By creating a vision of yourself, you can align your goals based on your values and principles. Your script should be based on your likes and dislikes, and your tastes and preferences.

It should be a story that defines your approach towards life. You have to decide whether it will be a story full of trying out new things, a proper direction towards what you do. Or should it be a story based on not achieving your goals and repeated failures.

You must think and introspect upon how you want to write your script. There are a few questions which you can think upon which may help you rewrite your life's script based upon your principle values.

1. What is it that you want to achieve the most before you die?
2. What are the top three things that are keeping you off track?
3. What is the most impactful thing that you will have when you achieve your goal?

4. How could you make this goal more specific and achievable?
5. What is the one thing you will do knowing that, by doing it you will not fail?
6. What is one change that you will like to bring in your life right now?
7. What change in your working method would you bring about so that it creates a major difference in your life?
8. Can you double the value of your goal?
9. What should you get rid of from your life right now?
10. What do you need to do to fully live your life?
11. Do you really want more to happen in your life? Do you get emotionally charged thinking about it?
12. What do you really want less to happen in your life? Do you get emotionally charged thinking about it?
13. Can you commit to achieving your goals right now?
14. Does your work make you happy? If yes, Why? If not, Why?
15. What is taking you closer or away from your goal? Can you list it?
16. What are the things that you really love?
17. What are the things that you really hate?
18. What are the changes in your life that will bring you towards getting more peace?

As you start answering these questions, you will be able to reevaluate your preferences in life. A sudden clarity towards your thoughts and in your vision will be the first thing that you will notice. If you visualize and list your goals based on this list, you will soon be moving on a path of creating a happy and a fulfilling life.

Working on one's own goals and vision needs clarity and focus. This list will help you attain that.

So instead of lazing around it is time to tie your shoelaces and hit the racetrack. Why delay the vision further if you know how to chart your path. What is now needed is just a decision to get to work. Like the Nike tag line says… Go get it!

4. What interferes in visualizing your goals?

Why is that moving towards your goals is so difficult and painstaking? Just thinking about the goals and dreams seems easier in the visualization process but it becomes difficult when one sets out to achieve it. The first problem that we encounter is that most of us don't know that what we are truly after, is true to our values or not?

The only way to solve this equation is to connect to your higher consciousness when visualizing your goals. Connecting to the higher awareness and intuition is a wise start to move towards achieving your goals.

Most of the goal setting experts talk about the various methods of visualization, but the hardest part is to take it easy. Getting our ego in between might hamper the process. Visualization should not be done forcefully. You cannot think of achieving your goals in an egoistic, loud, forceful manner. It might get you emotionally charged for a moment, but will get you away from your true and deep emotional values. Adding force to the visualization process will do nothing but tire you out. Avoid it.

Instead, visualizing your goals should be a part of your intuitional, introspective and calm state of mind. It should come naturally and easily. Such level of visualizing is rather encouraging and it helps you build your self-confidence. Instead of forcefully trying to control things, you gently begin to trust yourself and begin to act upon it. Also when it comes naturally, and not through your egoistic self, it gives you a clear view of how to act in the best manner to deal with the current situation. This in turn will make you a more confident person and your intuition and visualization will soon become your second nature.

Once you know the difference between your egoistic and your natural self, a dramatic change ensues. You then know the real difference between holding on and letting go of something. Once you start to let go of the things that seem to be forceful, the power of intuition begins to grow. This is the true power of intuition that influences your reality. Changing your attitude on the inside, by letting go of your egoistic self will help you achieve what you truly want from the outside.

There is no magic potion or a wand to be used when it comes to achieving your goals. Simply aligning your values based on your power of intuition will get you closer to your goals. It is more of a spiritual process which you can try out.

Also if we get too attached to the result, we may get the ego back into action. This again will make the goal setting process seem like a chore and will make you tired. The best example of concentrating on the process and not forcing yourself to achieve the goal is clearly explained in the Bhagwad Geeta. We should not get the ego to cloud our vision to achieve what we want. This forceful action is often based on the emotion of fear than of anything else. Due to this we also put too much focus on what we don't have which leaves us in a vicious circle.

Your goal should be to aim on building your strengths based on your intuition and your natural ability to visualize your goals. It might be a little difficult in the beginning, but once it becomes second nature, achieving your accomplishments becomes easy. The only thing that we need to remember is not to let our ego to come in between.

5. What Parents and Children can do together?

What can an eight year old girl teach me about goal setting? Or is it that I can teach her? My daughter Aashi is eight and she has been setting the best example of the method of goal setting that I have seen. Almost a month before her birthday, she sits down to make lists. Her birthday list is very specific with the types of gifts that she wants, and who will be sending them to her.

Once she has her birthday gift sorted, Aashi gets busy making lists of the guests she would like to have on her birthday. She also lists down the games, the theme, and the type of invite that she expects to be sent, the dress code, and the games that she will be playing with her friends. Too much for an eight year old to do? Not at all…

Then comes the interesting part. She then writes down the number of days left for her birthday and pastes it next to her birthday list. She then simply cuts a date with a pen every morning when she wakes up, letting her know how many days are left for her birthday.

When it comes down to goal setting, making lists and looking forward to achieving them is the best thing that we can teach our children to do.

The easiest way we can teach our children the methods of goal setting is by encouraging them to get involved in tasks where they have things to do based on a timeline. An upcoming birthday party is a fun example of that. This also applies to the other events that may come up in their life.

We should suggest our children to attach a timeline to their task based on their abilities and the goal that they want to attain. Children must understand that deadlines are important. Set a good example and your children will follow. They learn best through examples that we set for them.

Showing your interest in helping the child in setting goals is the best you can do for them to see results quickly. They need proper support and guidance from their parents to do so. You can teach them this method by making them write down their goals and make them work towards achieving it. Drawing of charts and illustrations of the things that they want to achieve is another interesting way of helping them achieve it. It is more like making kids create their own vision board.

Such actions when taken with the help and support of the parents, help kids prepare for adulthood. The parents must make the kids realize that goal setting is important and that they need to practice goal setting over and over again till they master it. As the kids grow old you can teach them to set goals on how to budget their own allowances in school. You can also teach them how to set health goals, etc. and how to communicate and work along with other people.

Teaching kids to set goals as early in their life is recommended for all the parents. Children who are properly guided with their goals since childhood are found to be successful individuals when they become adults. When parents teach their children on how to set goals and to be organized, this in turn helps the children do the same for themselves, when they grow up. They are the future generation. It is the responsibility of the parents to nurture and guide them so that they have a better tomorrow.

❑

Chapter 2

Setting Goals

"Our goals can only be reached through a vehicle of a plan, in which we must fervently believe, and upon which we must vigorously act. There is no other route to success."

– Pablo Picasso

1. A rock star lost behind the desk

Every one of us, at some point of life wants to live like a rock star. A rock star here means someone who gets to live life on his terms. Someone who gets to do what he or she wants, dealing with things the way they want to.

But how is it possible that most of us 'To-be-Rock stars' end up behind the office desk? How they get lost in the accounting spreadsheets and end up living boring lives, doing dull office work?

On one side, we have dreamt of a successful career, based on our terms. Whereas on the other side, we find ourselves entering boring data in our office laptops.

Well, here are the reasons behind it. Most of this happens because we do not have a clearly defined goal in our life.

Worse, we don't even know what we need to do even if we have a specific clear goal.

It means that if you have decided to become rich and financially free, even that is not enough. You should know what needs to be done to become financially free and independent. You should have the realization of the time and effort you need to invest in order to achieve financial freedom.

You should be willing to pay the price of getting successful. Also you should be in a state of mind where you are enjoying the work you are doing.

In the same way, if you hope to become a rock star, then you might want to think about how you actually intend to make that happen. Why is being a 'Rock star' so important for you and how are you going to make it happen? What would you pay for it?

While you do make all these decisions, you also need to ensure that this is truly what you're passionate about. That your intended goal is something that you always enjoy thinking about, enjoy working on and just can't wait to see it turn to reality.

There are so many people in this world who do not get the success that they want due to lack of clarity of achieving their goals.

It is their incapability of proper decision making that when happened repeatedly in several situations gets them the same unsuccessful results. Depending upon the individual nature of the person, one should keep some basic idea of how to develop one's ability to solve problems more efficiently. This attitude will help one make sensible and sound decisions.

Of course, the techniques given in the next section simply provide that, particularly when someone needs to conclude that they not only work well for them, but can also benefit others.

2. Easy and Simple Decisions, How to Make Them?

Quite often, we fail to know the difference between a decision and an opinion. Opinions are easy, they lack firmness and responsibility. Decisions are firm. They have accountability and are a product of sound judgment. Having an opinion about something and making a decision about something are two different things altogether.

Yesterday a rather unfortunate incident happened at our workplace. We came across a recorded conversation of one of our current employees talking to an ex-employee we had sacked from our company a few months ago. The reason of letting the ex-employee go was simply because his method of working was incongruent to the values of the company. While the conversation continued, the Ex-employee started to show disrespect towards most of the members of our team, accusing them of doing office politics against him. Soon all the team members who came across the recorded conversation were enraged and started hurling abuses at the ex-employee. So much so that they wanted to meet him face to face. I don't know what could have happened next.

Being on the senior position, me and my partner had to pacify everyone and had to make them let go of the matter. Slowly everyone started to get back to work but somewhere it ruined everyone's day.

Such events if left unattended can not only hamper a day's work, it can have people end up with serious unpleasant consequences.

How we deal with such situations is to make decisions then and there keeping our emotions in check while focusing the larger picture.

Many times we are required to make decisions based on the data that we have been provided. Usually that data is also not enough to make a sound judgment. But we may have to take our decisions based on the data and options provided. This decision should be based on all the choices that have been provided to us. When we come to a conclusion, it should be based on sound evaluation of the alternatives available to us.

There are situations in your life where you have to make quick decisions. Being a leader you are required to be quick and less critical, while being able to analyze the big picture at the same time. If acted quickly, without paying attention to the overall impact of the situation can result in certain ramifications which sooner or later affects the actions for the worst.

An impulsive decision often ends up in the wrong thing. Your decision making skills will be put to the test throughout these situations, so it would be best if you truly consider all their inputs prior to making an unbiased conclusion on that particular concern. Hearing everyone's opinion but doing what you feel is best for every one is the best piece of action that you can take in any critical situation.

Why this section is important in this book of setting goals is that it is your duty to keep your GPS in check. Building a roadmap towards your goals will have various checkpoints on your way where you will have to focus and guide yourself and your teams focus.

Now the most important point before making any impulsive decision is this. Simply ask yourself this one question, "Does this help you get closer to your goals?"

I repeat this as a reminder for you to ask this question now and again. Any action you take in your life, be it a major life decision or a simple one, like buying something, ask yourself this. The simplest way to decide if it is a good idea or not, is to ask yourself, if it will help you to accomplish your goals?

The decision is going to take you nearer or further from your goals. It will change your way of thinking while analyzing for and against it.

If you are really out to achieve something, acting on this question will help you keep your emotions in check and will help you realign your focus. Always and always, make this way of thinking your priority.

Just find out what your passion is, keep looking at the bigger picture in mind and keep moving. If you love what you're working upon, you will embrace everything that needs to be done for it, and that too in a rightful way.

3. Use the Magnifying Glass

Do you remember the first time you had seen through a magnifying glass? Suddenly you begin to see an enlarged image of everything you see through it. Much like the zoom lens on your phone, only difference is that even though there is no major sci-fi technology involved, you as a child get enchanted by the view that feels more alive.

You see things clearly and much larger in size. As a child, do you remember roaming around the room, focusing it and looking at different objects through it?

I remember zooming in on my palm to see my fingerprints. Also looking through it to see if there is any speck of dirt on my palm. Also I would zoom through it on all the nearby articles I could find, currency notes were the most interesting, I was often intrigued by the various patterns on the surface of the note. Often carefully looking at the design and the salient pattern a note holds.

But this moment of exploration usually doesn't last very long. After you have spent some time looking at various things through the magnifying glass, you don't usually stop at that. We all know that further we move the glass away from the object, the larger it becomes. We often try zooming it to the max by taking the glass as further as possible. It reaches a point where the objects image cannot be zoomed any further and it turns either blurry or gets distorted into an abstract form. This is point where we lose our focus. We often do this while viewing at different goals in our adult life also, that too on a regular basis.

Imagine looking at the many goals in your life through your magnifying glass and stretching your view to the point where you lose focus.

This is something that we need to ask ourselves every day. What are we desiring and what are we focusing upon?

You are what you focus upon. You become what you focus upon.

This alone determines what and where will you end up in your life.

Now here is a little secret. If we focus on helping others achieve their dreams and desires, we have a mighty chance of achieving ours as well. It is only a matter of changing your focus.

The moment you start giving attention to the task that needs to be completed with complete honesty and diligence, things start turning in your favor.

Whenever we start concentrating and thinking upon a particular task or thing with undiverted attention, we get closer to our goal. Our minds get easily distracted by the not so important things around us today. Today's technology around us creates 'noise' which is enough to keep us distracted from getting what we need to achieve.

We, once tired of all this noise end up focusing on self and start living a life with a little bit of selfish and self-absorbed demeanor. Once we become self-absorbed, we cannot grow any more. We need to look outside of ourselves to realize what is holding us from succeeding.

If you sometimes think that nothing is happening in your favor, it's time to rethink. Maybe you are self-absorbed! The only way out is to focus upon the tasks you do with undivided attention. Yet at the same time, you should not be too self-absorbed as to not see the bigger or the holistic view of your task.

The best way to do this is to start paying attention to the right things. Start connecting with the right people. People who are smarter that you will always help you in deciding where to put your focus upon. Also the smart lot will teach you how to set a holistic view towards your goals.

Focusing on the right things, with the right mindset, surrounded by the right people will automatically make you happier from inside. Don't forget that you are a product of your attention and this is what you will become. Knowing what to focus upon will also remove all the negative focus you can have on other things.

4. Learn How to set S.M.A.R.T. Goals

Most of the time, people think of goal setting as extra work and behave as if they don't have time for it. Every individual in his life has his own individual goals, family goals, money goals, business goals, etc. But we are so engrossed in our day to day life that we don't realize that we are losing on time, which in turn makes us lose sight of our various life goals. The only method to get out of this mindset is to make goal setting as a priority and to consider all the obstacles in your life as stepping stones towards your goals. You should know how to make the best of each situation and not get too consumed by your work and by your responsibilities towards your family that you get little time for personal enrichment of any kind.

One approach towards goal setting is that you can set goals together as family. This helps keep each other accountable for their deeds and prevent you from going off track. Also the joy that you might get from accomplishing a goal as a family becomes a matter of pride and admiration. The best way to set goals either as an individual or as a family is the S.M.A.R.T. way. Setting S.M.A.R.T. goals keeps your focus aligned and helps you measure the level and extent of the goal that you want to achieve.

Specific

This goal has to gel with your personality and character. Most people set vague goals like I want to lose weight or I want to learn the piano. This usually does not work in the long run.

Specific goals written on paper with full details will get you closer to attaining them. Something like "I will lose 10 kilos by January next year" or "I will attend 2 hours of piano classes every week" have more chances of being completed than their vague counterparts.

It is always better to be detailed in terms of numbers, date and other such specifications that you need to mention to attain your goals.

Measurable

Say for example you want to earn more money or you need to add a more clients to your workforce. It is always better to mention the number of clients or the amount of money that you want to earn. The more specific you are in numbers, the easier it will be for you to calculate the factors that you need to complete your goal. Goals need to be measurable so that you can keep track of how well you are doing. It can be the number of working hours, the number of calories you intend to burn during your morning jog, etc. Anything that is measurable is more likely to be achieved and accomplished.

Attainable

All the goals that you set should also fall in this category. Just blind promises to yourself, will never work. Going outside your comfort zone in order to achieve something is an intelligent move. But promising yourself something rather unattainable is more of a joke than goal setting. Vowing to earn million dollars in 24 hours while you are jobless and broke at the same time is not a goal. It is waiting for a miracle. Instead, focusing on something attainable as going for meetings and effective job hunting etc. is what is more attainable and thus, has to be followed in this manner.

Relevant

The goal you set should also be relevant to your mission. It should match and blend with your vision, at the same time it should be relevant. For example, if you set a goal of becoming the Prime Minister of the country and you have no interest in politics, it would be a rather irrelevant goal to accomplish. The goals you set should gel with your persona and character.

Time-Bound

All your goals should have a timeline attached to it. Having an exact time and date will spur you to start working on your goals, instead of putting it off for another day. Keeping a time line can be something like "I will give 90 minutes of undivided attention to my children every day." Or something like "I will work out in the gym at least 5 days in a week". Attaching a specific date is the key element in such types of goals.

Every time you set a S.M.A.R.T. goal for yourself, you make clear, sound decisions which serve as a roadmap for you to pursue your goals. Using the S.M.A.R.T. method will help you accomplish your goals with ease and clarity.

5. This Should Be Your Number One Goal

Every aspect of your life is equally important. So are having goals in every category so that you have a happy and balanced life. But have you ever thought of what the most important category in your life is and what should be your number one goal? Needless to say, the most important category is that of your health. Any goal set in this category is nothing but a number one goal.

Now how do you evaluate your health and set health goals, you may ask? First and foremost, you need to know where you stand right now. The best way to evaluate the heath in an individual is to get regular annual health checkups. This is especially important for people above 40. This should include your blood test, weight, cholesterol, etc. Everything once tested should be noted and tracked from here on.

The next step here is to check whether your weight, cholesterol levels, etc. fall under the normal range. Once you know where you stand, and the normal range, you can decide which category you need to work upon. This can be done with the help of your family doctor. Once this is done, it is the time to work on your health goals.

Why, you may ask, that I need to have heath goals?

Because you cannot do anything without good health. It's so essential to be physically and mentally able to do the work you need to do, in order to achieve your goals.

Any minor ailment, like a normal headache can get you

off track for a couple of hours. It drains you completely, hampering your physical and mental wellbeing.

A bad health condition kills your productivity and creativity. Our bodies are busy fighting against the bacteria and virus in and around us. But when our immunity gives in and we fall sick, the illness affects our thinking and judgment. Such things create obstacles in our lives. Illnesses also hamper our speed of getting things done.

This often leads us to feel low and demotivated. In such a state of mind, one's efficiency is seriously hampered.

With low energy levels and poor immunity, we aren't motivated to get things done. Poor health also increases the stress level of our bodies. It creates a demand on the body to create normalcy. It takes extra effort for the body to function with increased blood pressure, increased stress hormones or with clogged arteries. Let us not forget the physical stress that the body goes through during any illness or ailment.

If at all we want to work well and enjoy every moment in our life, being in good health should be our optimum priority.

Even addictions like smoking and consuming alcohol can cause enough damage to the body as to hamper our productivity. It might look cool in the workplace, but smoking can lead to some serious consequences in the long run. What will you do of achieving your goals if you don't have a body fit enough to enjoy your achievements?

We should not forget that when it comes to good health, if we want to have the best, we should be the best that we can be.

We need to be bold enough to accept and come out of our addictions. Also we must take charge of our bodies and strive towards world class fitness. Striving towards a fit and healthy body in itself is a goal one should pursue with the fullest of attention and intention.

6. The Recipe for financial goal setting

When it comes to financial success, many people get uncomfortable with the concept of setting goals. They don't know how to go about it. People often try looking for shortcuts and simple ways to make money. Making money is not enough. We need to know the process, as well as respect the concept of retaining, and spending money.

Some people are excellent at making money, but they are extremely poor at retaining it. Some are excellent retainers, but poor givers. Money if not shared, or put to work, starts to decline. Financial goal setting, works differently for everyone. It does not have a fixed recipe. What works for me, might not work for you. Each of us has to customize the recipe according to ones needs and temperament.

Have you ever wondered why this system works differently for different people? Well, there may be three reasons.

Let's say your main goal is to earn 10 lakh rupees a month. You always strive for it and often think on how to get to earn that income. Now let's compare your situation to an athlete who wants to run a 22 kilometer marathon. This marathon runner also spends time on the tracks with the same diligence and dedication that you do. So much for the analogy. Now if someone asks the runner who he identifies himself as, he will very confidently reply that he is a marathon runner. This runner, even if he has not succeeded in running a good 22 kilometers, still identifies himself as one. He lives that role, convinced since the very beginning that he is a runner, and he looks at everyone from that perspective only. Whether or not, he may be able to run and win a 22 kilometer marathon, he will always identify himself as a marathon runner. Moreover, he will be happy and proud with his identity, and will carry himself with that air of confidence in him.

Now think of this, if you haven't earned that 10 lakh rupees income as yet, will you be as confident as the marathon runner? Will you have that same air of confidence that he has? Also, if someone asks you what you do, will you give him a similar reply that you are a businessman who is on his way to earn his 10 lakh rupees a month goal?

If you don't identify yourself with what you are, it becomes incongruent to your nature. This is the first factor that keeps you away from achieving your financial goal.

Another factor that needs to be considered in your financial goals is that of accuracy, and lack of clarity. If you decide that you need to make more money in business, it's simply not enough. Where is the clarity in this statement? Suppose you come up with a number, and say that you want to make 10 lakhs rupees a month. This is better than the previous statement, but even this is not clear enough. Just by giving it a number, does not mean that you can achieve the goal. Like we had discussed earlier, your statement should be emotionally driven, and should have a plan of action. Only then will something tangible happen.

Setting up a goal for yourself, should be as accurate as you saying, " I will make X amount of money, working everyday on Y, for a consistent Z amount of hours every day, in order to get closer to my goals." Such statements when emotionally driven, work as a catalyst in your pursuit in goal setting.

Also adding a reward for yourself, after completing the goal, boosts it further. So once you get what you want, don't forget to reward yourself with something that you love.

Lastly, the factor of being incongruent with your field of action also affects your financial status. I can give you a personal example in this context. My parents, being doctors, always wanted me to get into medicine. Though I myself was hardly interested in being a doctor myself. I'm very fortunate to have such open minded parents who understood me and let me pursue the field of my interest. Since I was good at drawing, and enjoyed working on it a lot, they let me get into College of Art, from where my journey towards Art direction began. Not many children get the chance I got. Very often do parents choose the career path for children? They hardly ever consider the interests or the inclination of their child, but focus only on the career they have chosen for their child. Their idea of a career is at times, entirely different from what a child will choose for himself.

Similarly, sometimes goals are just "forced" upon us. This usually happens in our workplaces. Goals are set for employees with the hopes of creating a sense of competition and morale, yet they fail to work. That's because the employers themselves don't identify with the goals and do their job just for the sake of doing it.

So, if you don't identify yourself with the goal, there are chances that you may never achieve it. If a goal is incongruent to your core principles, you may never have your heart in it. The better way is to have your self-image accept the goal and work upon it.

The trick here is to imagine being the kind of person, who would most likely achieve that kind of goal. Then try being that person. Once you believe that kind of person is you, then you're ready to envision the outcome. You must then engage yourself in tasks that will push you past your comfort zone, enough to stretch you, to become the person you believe can achieve that kind of financial success.

For example, if you're a type of person who wants to learn how to make money through stocks, take a look at the people who are actually succeeding by investing in stocks, and study their actions. Get into their shoes and live their life. Envision yourself acting like these people. The difference between "being" and "trying to be" soon vanishes. Set your goal setting actions to strengthen your skills, to be more like the people you want to be.

"To be", is the secret to financial success. You do this, and you automatically, come closer to achieving your goals.

❑

Chapter 3

Writing Your Goals

Write it down. Written goals have a way of transforming wishes into wants; cants into cans; dreams into plans; and plans into reality. Don't just think it - ink it.

—Michael Korda

1. The Quick and Easy Goal Setting Method

Many people fail in their journey towards goal setting. This happens due to two reasons. One, they do not know the proper process and the methods of goal setting. Second, even if they know the method, they do not implement it in their daily lives.

These methods should be practiced so much so that they become your second nature. Only a proper goal setting method, when practiced on a fairly regular basis can really help you to achieve and fulfil your dreams and aspirations.

Most people usually fail to understand such methods and realize their mistakes once time has passed. It is when the year ends, many people realize that they have not achieved most of the things that they had set out to achieve for the year.

One method is to sit quietly with yourself and decide upon the things that how you would like each part of your life to be. It should be more of an inner discussion with yourself, where you can sit and think upon your life's priorities.

The proper way to set goals for yourself all starts with having a discussion with yourself and reflecting inwardly and determining what you want each part of your life to be. It should cover all the areas of your life that you would like to change.

Broadly spoken, it can be areas of your relationships, health, finances, business, etc. Over time these are the things that when worked upon will make maximum impact upon your personal wants and needs.

Talking to yourself, might feel a bit weird in the beginning, but it is the best method for self-reflection. Setting aside some time for yourself, without any outward distractions and thinking about your goals and achievements is the best method to start this process. The next step is to note your thoughts on a clean piece of paper.

You can begin with writing about where you see yourself in the current time in each of the areas that you have thought of. Then it is time to make a parallel note where you should mention what you would like to change about those areas of your life and why you want those changes. Then it is wise to set a realistic timeline with it, mentioning how much time you would need to accomplish each of your goals.

Writing your goals on paper, turns it into a commitment. Any unwritten goal is not a goal, it is a wish. Wishes don't come with commitments. Neither do they come with a timeline or a date. And not all wishes are meant to be fulfilled.

Physically writing down your goals on paper, is like a contract that you make with yourself to complete your goals. This contract is capable of motivating you to move ahead towards completing it. Also adding a reason of why you want to complete your goal, binds you emotionally with it. Once written in this manner, it is not a mere statement anymore. All this is not a thought in your mind, it has turned into a commitment which now demands an actionable step. Adding a time frame to your goals keeps you committed to getting it completed within the given time.

Also, you need to keep this list where you can see it quite often. This keeps you aware of your commitment and you continue acting upon it. If you don't keep it near you, you might forget all about it.

The advantage of this method is that it keeps you aware of where you are in different areas of your life and keeps you motivated enough to improve it. Writing is the best method to get your thoughts on paper and to make it actionable.

2. What you must have known earlier!

If you set a map of your life and follow it in the right way, you win. The key idea behind success is to have such victories, and grow. So, the thing to do here is to make plans and to keep working on them constantly. It should always be like a ship with a rudder, a great motor and enough fuel. Now if this ship is maneuvered correctly, it is bound to reach its destination. If you really want to get somewhere, or achieve something, all obstacles, large or small are nothing but silly work that keeps you busy. They should not stop you from advancing towards that something or somewhere.

Whereas, if we quit our search on the way, it is losing. Losing, in other words ids permanently quitting something. Indeed, we must never quit even when loss happens, we must just change approaches. If, at all we do lose, we must begin again, more intelligently.

Sure, in some ways, I am saying that winning is everything that a goal is, and losing is nothing but the temporary obstacles on the way to the winning if understood in the right ways. There is no replacement to genuine and permanent victory, whatever it costs. When you use a genuine approach, and get to where you want to, that's real victory.

Some people stop after succeeding at a single goal. That is not enough. The understanding of true success is that one must continue working upon his goals. He must continue doing what's necessary to get to his aim.

One simple thought that one must know while he is on

his journey to success is that he should not set goals just for the heck of achieving it. It also matters that the reason why one wants to achieve something is always more important that the goal itself. It does not matter whether you look good doing something, or you are admired by everyone else for your achievements. What is more important is the reason why you feel good after achieving your goals. It may be your self-worth. It may be your own satisfaction. The reason can be anything that you identify with.

It can even be something that you have done, only to prove it to yourself that you are capable of achieving it. This "Why" should be so strong enough for you to feel self-worthy and satisfied?

If we understand this clearly, and achieve our goals based on this criteria, this is pure victory. Without this, we will certainly lose. For a genuine victory, remember to have a genuine "Why" behind your goals. Without this reason, you can never be an expert in what you do.

Once you have a strong "Why", it alone is capable enough to help you cross one obstacle after the other, till you become a master of your field. This is genuine success. Strive for genuineness and keep at it till it becomes second nature to you. This is the secret that you need to know on your journey to success.

3. Now, when will you be happy?

"This house sucks. This society sucks. We deserve a better place." These are the words I used to tell my wife eight years ago, when we lived in an apartment in a not-so-good neighborhood. I often ended up my conversation with sentences like, "Once we move into a new house, we will be happy." I want you to think upon this statement for a moment. Doesn't this sound absurd, me and my wife, postponing our happiness, till we move into another house. Does it make sense to you?

This happens to everyone, sometime or the other. Think of it, there are so many people who say similar things like, "I will be happy once I get this promotion," or "Let me once get this deal, and then things will be fine. We will be happy again."

Do you know what we do when we say such things? We are just instructing our subconscious to postpone our happiness for some future time. Unfortunately, your subconscious mind does not have a mind of its own. It just knows how to follow orders. It only knows how to say "Yes" to everything. Once you say this statement, your subconscious simply say I Agree and starts working to make you unhappy. It believes in everything that you say or feel about yourself. And before you realize, you have self-sabotaged yourself in this process.

Your own subconscious will never let you be happy till you realize your mistake. Now the best way to overcome this is to realize that it is your conversation with yourself that will make or break your self-image.

Never forget that you must believe in yourself in order

to achieve these goals. In the majority of cases, the most effective tool is the use of affirmations. An affirmation made in a positive sense in the present tense, always works. Our subconscious, loves affirmations. If said in a believable, positive way, the subconscious listens to it and replies in its usual "Yes" and starts to live with it. For example, if you feel you need to become a better writer to achieve your goals, an affirmation might be, "I am a talented writer, who enjoys his writing, and my readers love my work."

Such affirmations work on things that you personally connect to. Try this with items that you feel you would like to personally pay more attention to, or get better at. Note that the statement is specific, positive and in the present tense.

It may sound funny but many people don't recognize success. They strive to achieve something, and once they get to it, they shift their goal to something more difficult and start to work upon achieving it. This goes on and on, sometimes for an entire lifetime. That brings up an interesting question. What is success? How do you, personally, define success? If you keep running after one thing or the other, your whole life, do you consider yourself to be successful? How do you measure your success? These are not questions just for the sake of it. Some never find success because they have not defined it nor identified what it looks and feels like. Hence, they are always in a striving mode. This is one reason why some folks don't enjoy their work. They never stop to smell the flowers and appreciate, by looking back at what they have achieved. Such folks hardly ever celebrate their victories. All pleasure for them is momentary, and they are always unhappy.

How about you? Where do you stand when it comes to happiness? How do you measure your achievements and celebrate the accomplishments you have already made? We are a society that values personal effort and expects individuals to succeed on their own.

As that is the case, it is up to you to clearly identify your goals. You have to imagine accomplishing it by clearly visualizing a very vivid picture of your success. Do it till you hear the "Yes" from your subconscious? It sounds strange, but it is better that you remaining unhappy throughout your life. Then you have to figure out the steps you will take, the obstacles that might get in the way, contingency plans, measurement metrics, etc.

Once you discover this, you will find yourself enjoying all your little victories as well as your bigger ones. Then you have to decide how you will celebrate your successes.

4. Have a Goalbook

When it comes to pursuing goals, we all know that the vast majority of people perform better if they have a visual aspect attached to their pursuit. If there is a visual element, with the goal, it becomes easier to follow it. The more vivid and clear it is, the better is the aim. Though, it is necessary to have an essential dream and a personal vision, having just goals is not enough. Apart from having important and relevant goals, having a plan and a mechanism to transform the goals into reality is equally important. If we attach a visual element, to our goal, it works like a blueprint for us and helps us get to our goals faster.

Rather than just coming up with a plan and memorizing its steps, it is better to put your goals on paper. World's renowned business coach and bestselling author Brian Tracy states, "Committing your goals to paper increases the likelihood of achieving those one thousand percent." It is for this reason that most great achievers have dreams that they visualize and which motivate them, hence create goals and then work on their action plan. Putting the goals on paper and referring to them on a repeated basis, helps you to know where you stand, thus guiding you in taking the necessary steps.

Writing your goals down, turns them into a visual element that works as a catalyst in your goal setting process. We should first make a broader list, of what we want to achieve, and then get down to the specifics of it. The next best thing that we can do is to discover the "Why" behind our quest. Once this is done, we should prioritize the elements in our list. The more important ones have to be worked upon first.

This plan that you have created, should be full of all the ideas that you can come up with in order to get what you want. This then arranged properly, will take the shape of the desired plan. Also don't forget to add any alternate plans that you have, if something doesn't work out as desired. These contingency plans are also a part of the master plan. Voila! Your Goalbook is ready.

The more detailed your Goalbook is, the easier it will become to follow your goals. Remember not to get too overambitious in writing your goals. Setting goals the S.M.A.R.T. way will help you get through this. Commit to these thoroughly and review these notes and ideas on a very regular basis. This will both motivate and refresh you on your personal journey.

Your Goal book will be your guide to success. What would it take for you to write down your goals? Research shows that people who do write down their goals are more likely to achieve them. They have a target, they know exactly what it looks like and they have a time line and an action plan on how they are going to get to their success. When was the last time you took a look at your goals like this?

5. Build it. One rep at a Time

Have you ever tried managing a lot of goals at the same time? I bet you might have felt exhausted after a while. When it comes to self-discipline, you can compare it to weight lifting. If we work out in the gym using lighter weights, we will not gain any muscle and all our exercise will get wasted. Similarly, if we try lifting extra kilos, more than we can handle, we are bound to get injured.

Similarly trying to run a 22 km marathon at once is not possible without any prior practice. You cannot just get up from your couch and start running a good 22 kilometers. You might feel fine in the beginning, but there is a huge chance of failure here.

When we set lot of goals at the same time, it is more like lifting heavy weights at once or more like running the marathon without any practice.

Have you ever attended a self-help session or a motivational seminar? It has been observed that majority of people come out motivated after a self-help class or a seminar. They are so emotionally charged, that they try to make rapid changes in their way of work. They try reforming every rule and ritual of their company. This happens till this burst of motivation ends. As soon as the initial charge wears off, all changes and reformations fall flat on the ground. Then organization and the staff, all come back to the same starting point, sometimes even for the worse. Unfortunately, no matter how much willpower to change one has, there is always a finite supply.

On a personal front, we often see this with chronic habits like overeating. If a person is stressed, he is bound to binge on an unwanted snack. However aware of himself or herself one is, the stress of losing weight is enough for a person to raid the refrigerator when one least needs it. The same happens with smoking. Smokers, who often vow to themselves to cut down on their cigarettes, often find themselves failing miserably, within a couple of hours. If one bout of stress can lead to someone to overeat or to smoke a cigarette, imagine how difficult it would be trying to achieve multiple goals at once.

The silver lining here is that even though will power is finite, we can increase its capacity by exercising it on a regular basis. If we practice self-control, on a regular basis for a few weeks, we are bound to show improvement than the few who have not practiced any self-control yet. For example, if we follow mindful eating for a few weeks and avoid snacking on junk food for a few weeks, it becomes easier and easier to follow this pattern as the days pass by.

The best way to go ahead is work on your goals in a gradual manner. Don't just jump into managing too many things at the same time. You might end up stressed and snacking in front of the refrigerator, with a cheese sandwich in your mouth. Focusing on one goal at a time, will definitely limit your distractions and will help you progress in a linear way. Working upon them in this manner, will help you see gradual improvements which will soon compound into major breakthroughs. That too without any unwanted stress.

You can start by working on a goal for a week or so. If you feel that it is getting easier for your system to accept the change, you can add another goal by the next week. Remember the weight lifting analogy, it has to happen step by step, not all at once.

❑

Chapter 4

First Steps

The first step towards getting somewhere is to decide that you are not going to stay where you are.

–Chauncey Depew

1. When to listen to loud music, and when not to

Let us talk about a young executive Gaurav, who hits the gym diligently three times a week. While he is very particular with this exercise regime, he often notices the lack of focus in other members of the gym. He often sees their workout is more to do with petty chit chatting than to do with actual exercise. Some of them are engrossed in their mobile phones, reading and texting messages. Some are seen roaming around and talking to each other, which often reduces their intensity and efficiency of their workouts.

He on the other hand, makes sure that his workouts are as effective as they intend to be. For this Gaurav has devised a rather unusual strategy.

He wears his earphones with music loud enough in his ears as to drown the unnecessary chatter in the gym. This helps him to improve his focus and he simply concentrates on his exercise regime. This simple act of putting on earphones significantly reduces his distractions, and he can effectively invest all his attention and energy on his exercise routine. By the time he is done with his workout, his clothes are dripping with sweat, while he feels both physically and emotionally satisfied.

On his way back home, Gaurav keeps his earphones aside, gets in his car, wears his seatbelt and ensures that he safely drives back home. This time he avoids listening to loud music totally. So much so that he turns down the volume of the car stereo significantly. Here while getting back home, safety is the prime concern.

This is a fine example of intelligence of this man. He knows what he wants out of these two situations and then he makes sure that he changes his routine to get the best out of both the situations. Such examples of wisdom lead a man to live his life, in such a way that he is not bothered by his surroundings and he simply concentrates on getting the most out of any situation.

Unfortunately in life, people state that they want to accomplish a goal but they don't start working on it. They keep moving their goals ahead due to external distractions. They keep making excuses looking for a better time to start and end up in procrastinating the task, only to find that another life event has come up. Soon delays start happening repeatedly, and the quest towards achieving the goals get lost somewhere. It is then, that people realize that they are at the wrong end of the road to success.

There is never a perfect time in our life to begin pursuing our goals. Start now. Now is the right time to begin. If we keep waiting for the right moment, soon we may see other things come up in between. These things and events will need our time and attention and soon we will forget our aim. Slowly will come a day when age will catch up. Then will be a time where we might regret our decision of not taking action at the right time.

Instead of getting into unwanted details, and getting yourself absorbed in mindless chatter, it is better to eliminate all the distractions and concentrate on achieving the desired result. We must remember that even small acts, when done with the right amount of concentration can lead to massive results. What are the tasks that you have been putting off since a while? Is it connecting with old friends? Is it finishing a desired educational course? Or is it about saving some money?

Follow the example of Gaurav. Get hold of your earphones that you can use to block out all the distractions and focus on the task ahead. This is the decision when you need to choose between being distracted by external factors, or to come out of it using your own innovative and unique methods. Doing some initial research and setting out small, first steps that, when continued to be done on a daily basis will lead you in the right direction. This is when you should set out to make the necessary adjustments in your lives, make a strong commitment to yourself about what you want to achieve, and set out to achieve them with full force.

2. Is being productive pulling you back?

As we make progress on our goal setting journey, we often have moments where we evaluate our success based on our productivity. Loosely said, productivity is the measurement of how much work you get done quickly. The better you are at getting things done, the more you are able to take on more jobs. This gets even better when we start making progress, towards achieving bigger and better goals. Getting things done quickly sets us on a fast lane to success.

But there is a catch here. Once you learn to do things fast, it gets addictive trying to do things even faster. It's like overlooking the details of certain things, just to tick them off on your to-do list.

If you know someone who is quite regular at handling to-do lists, you may observe, that the person is happier ticking things off from the list, just for the heck of it. It doesn't matter to them if they are absorbing the information, the task is providing to them.

It gets hazardous for someone who is a high school kid preparing for an exam. Let's take Taniya's example. Taniya is in high school and is preparing for her board exams this year. What is expected of her is that she is supposed to cover the major part of the syllabus, while learning and comprehending what she has read on her way. If Taniya, starts ticking off the chapters of her book one by one, just to get it off her list, and doesn't bother understanding the basics of what the syllabus explains, it's going to be a major disaster when she sits down to give her exams.

Just to brush through chapters so one can check things off is a poor choice to make. It applies to every area of goal setting. It makes us feel that we are making progress. But, even though it may feel that we have worked towards it, the results are going to be bad.

Taking shortcuts, just to finish a number of tasks quickly is a strict no-no. Sometimes, we begin our day with a really large number of tasks on our to-do lists. It can be overwhelming just looking at their quantity. Then we are tempted to do the easier tasks first, just to get them checked off the list. Also, the easiest ones take the least amount of time, so it seems better to do them, rather than getting stuck with completing a larger task.

What if those easy tasks are low priority, low impact tasks? Coming back to Taniya's example, what is more productive for her? To cover ten easy chapters, or one difficult one is the question?

Sometimes you have to do several easier tasks as part of an overall bigger task. What if Taniya comes across a question in mathematics that demands a sequentially deducted answer? Maybe she might have to solve some easy equations in the beginning, and the get to the difficult one. Maybe these easy equations are important to get you to the final solution. Sometimes those easier tasks are important for your overall goals.

Here, the important thing that makes you truly productive

is not the size of the task. Also, being productive does not depend on how easy or difficult the task is. It is to be working on the right things at the right time.

What is important here is that what impact your task has on the overall goal you are trying to achieve. Like in Taniya's case, it's the overall impact of the easier questions that will result in solving the final complicated equation. So what's important here is to decide what the most important task at the time is, and to work upon it. You have to decide the impact of the task in hand and whether it will make the other tasks easier. Also, the sequence it should be done in, before you move on to the next task.

Suppose Taniya is giving her mathematics exam and she comes across two problems that demand the same amount of attention, and are of the same weightage, what do you think she should do first? Should she do the easier one first, and then move on to the next one, that obviously demands more time to solve? Or should she decide upon solving the difficult one first, giving it enough time it needs, and quickly finish the easier one, before she submits her examination sheet to the examiner?

This makes it a little trickier, but the solution is for you to decide. What would you suggest Taniya to do first? Should it be the easier one, that she is confident in completing in less time, or the difficult one, that demands more attention? My advice here is that she should do the difficult one first, this is where temptation is the greatest. Here, you should always tackle the bigger task. It's far too easy to put it off because it's a large task. It is only if you are short of time, should you use the other alternative.

When we just do the easier things first, just to check them off, for the adrenaline rush it gives, is a trap you should avoid failing into. This is where we often let the difficult tasks be the way they are because they demand more time and effort. It gets to be like an addiction, because we tell ourselves we're really making progress. Whereas, in reality, we're just going on and on doing the same thing over and over again. This is not what productivity means.

3. What can you unlearn from a Piglet?

The animal world is full of wonders. Especially in the pig world. As soon as a piglet is born, strange and quick transformation begins to take place. The piglet is up on his feet and starts wobbling around mamma pig within an hour of being born.

The problem is when you are a human and not a piglet. This is where change takes time. For example, if you decide to learn a new skill, say learn a new language or learn cooking, you might wonder that why is it taking so much time? You might get surprised by the amount of time you need to invest in order to learn this skill.

Remember you are not a piglet.

Change in the human world requires patience. What you may think is a long time, may just be a few weeks of practice lessons in real time. Fortunately or unfortunately, humans take years to learn and to perfect new behaviors.

Let us assume that you are trying your hand at dancing. You might have been inspired by watching videos and shows related to dance and decided to give it a try. Initial few weeks would be exciting where you would have spent some time learning a few steps. But then after a few weeks, the plateau phase sets in. You might start looking at yourself in the mirror and get frustrated at no substantial growth happening. This can be rather disheartening, keeping in mind the dream that you have envisioned for yourself.

But let us not forget, that the dancers in the videos that you have been watching are not just chance dancers. They have been practicing their moves for quite some time now and have been working on their dancing skills for years. Also, there might be a team of dance coaches and choreographers involved in the act so that they can help them give their best performance on screen. Seeing them dance and comparing your moves with them, will definitely question your dancing skills.

Well, the brighter side of the equation is that it takes time and practice, but you will eventually get there. What may seem like an unachievable trait, can be developed in a matter of few years of practice.

We must understand that any change that we want to happen in our lives, cannot happen NOW. It usually takes a minimum of 21 days to get the behavior into a new routine. After that it is all a matter of practice.

Then, it also depends on your natural inclination towards it. Only if you are genuinely interested in developing the new habit, will you give it the time necessary for it to grow.

Now that you have decided to alter a behavior, learn a new skill, or modify the way you allocate your time, start with a small step, that you're confident you can achieve.

Patience is the key. One cannot see self-transformation in a moment. It takes time. Simply building up a distraction free environment around you, with no phones or computers to distract you, will start to create a difference. Setting aside time daily, preferably on the same time of the day is another tip that should be followed to work on any given habit.

Then it is a matter of focus, instead of trying to learn all the dance moves together, it would be better to start from one dance style at a time. Slowly, when you have practiced and developed your skills enough, can you move towards another dancing style. This method when followed, will keep you encouraged, and will get you across your plateau phase. With each style and move that you have practiced, will you see your confidence growing?

Now it's up to you to decide. What is that one skill that you want to master? What is that change that you want to see in your life? Once you have decided this, you can start working on it step by step. Joining a beginners course, starting to take weekend classes, are such examples of starting bit by bit.

If you still feel that you are not growing as much as you want to, try making the process even simpler by breaking it into sub goals. These can be smaller bits of the bigger goals that you want to achieve.

Slowly, you will be seeing yourself, transform into an expert. The skill that you had found so difficult to learn will slowly become second nature. You never know, that slowly you might be admired by the people around you for what, you once thought was impossible for you to learn. You may get jealous of the piglet for learning his skills so quickly. But remember, you are not a piglet. Change takes time. It is only a matter of patience and persistence.

4. Should I do it tomorrow?

Many tasks if put off till tomorrow will often hamper your growth. What can be done today, if left over to be done till tomorrow will simply pile upon each other and will lead you to end up nowhere? Also the time that you lose will never come back to you again. Why think of too many tomorrows, and delay the task that you can take care of today.

Nothing is more exhausting and tiring than keeping an incomplete task hanging over your head since eternity. If you procrastinate, it slowly starts taking you backwards instead of you moving towards the direction of your success. It starts with putting off the task for tomorrow that should have been taken care of yesterday. Instead of waiting for tomorrow to start something, the best way to move ahead is to just begin. This is the first secret to beat procrastination.

Also, no one, not even you, knows what is going to happen ahead. We can only guess and speculate the things and events that will happen tomorrow. The best way to move ahead is to seize the day right away, at the very present moment. This comes once we truly realize the value of time. It just needs no laziness and no idleness from our side.

There may be times when one is feeling unwell or something urgent has come up, that may not let you complete your given task. It may also happen that you may have to postpone your task due to some other important matter that you may have to deal with before completing the given task. If neither of this is the case, then postponing the task is simply the case of idleness and procrastination.

Often postponing or putting off a deadline for later can be bad for the end result of the work. We all know that when such time comes one ends up working carelessly, making errors and taking silly shortcuts thereafter. Also sitting down to work in such a situation is often full of panic and chaos.

Today, and only today is the time to do the right thing. Whenever there is a goal, a target, a job to be done, nothing is a better time than to do it today itself. Tomorrows are always meant for the next task that will come to you the next day.

5. Your sixty seconds of spontaneity!

We all know that if we get into every detail of any task and overly ruminate upon every work we do, we can end up losing other opportunities. Indecisive action does nothing more than taking us nowhere.

One way of thinking and evaluating our priorities in life is to sit and make a quick list of the major things we need in life. If we simply start thinking in a quick and intuitive manner, we can identify our genuine goals. If we simply sit down for a minute, and think spontaneously, with a clean and intuitive mind, we can easily identify our needs and goals… That too based on the order of priority.

The key to this is to be spontaneous and honest with yourself. The ideas that you do not believe in will not work for you, even if you try forcing it to work in your favor.

If you are bold enough to make the move, it just needs just sixty seconds to identify the opportunity and to make the move. We will miss all the opportunities that come our way if we don't identify ourselves with them. But only the truly genuine ones, that we consider to be good for us are the ones that need to be identified and to be acted upon. This is where saying 'maybe' and 'maybe not' will never work in your favor. It has to be a 'yes' and a 'no' and your judgment should be honest and sound enough to know the difference. If you are intuitive enough, with a clean heart, any opportunity can be converted into a golden harvest.

There will be times when you may have doubts. But the

want for the goal should be strong enough to get you through all the obstacles. All you need to say is a sure shot 'yes' to give it your best.

Giving your best in every situation is one such example of going ahead with full honesty. This helps in eliminating all the negative thought and impurities that come along with any difficult task. Based on our intuitive abilities, we should be ready to drop all the negativity that comes with any difficult or challenging task.

Now is the time to be patient and let all your aspirations turn into reality. Know this, you will ultimately reach your goals, just the way you want to, if you approach it with genuineness and never quit attitude at the same time. Success is nothing but a list of goals that have worked right for you.

6. When slowing down, try considering this…

There are two types of goals in the goal setting process, the easy ones and the difficult ones. When we talk about difficult ones, they are obviously more demanding. They need careful planning, and a lot of effort to execute. We need to stretch out of our comfort zone and need to give the best of our abilities to achieve them.

Then come the easier ones. These are the ones we reckon are easy to achieve and that they don't need much of planning and energy. In fact, if the goals are so easy, there is no point for you to add them to your goal setting list. Why bother for them anyway? But is it the right thing to do? Let's look at a simple example to explain this.

My daughter, at eight years old, is very good at sketching and drawing for her age. She enjoys every bit of her time when she engages in drawing. Most of her sketches are detailed and impressive, and need a lot of patience and practice. People often consider learning to draw, a very complicated task to achieve. But the truth is this, it's not as difficult. What it needs is continuous practice with a lot of interest. In my daughter's case, as she continued practicing, she began showing tremendous improvement in her lines and strokes. As the strokes improved, appreciation started coming from everyone who saw her sketches. This appreciation, gave her the energy and motivation to do more. Also, the sense of self satisfaction that she got from being able to draw what she wanted, fueled up her talent even further. Now she is on a path that if pursued diligently will take her towards mastery.

In the case of learning drawing, you cannot measure your progress in numbers. There is no method to measure your progress. It's all relative. In my daughter's case, if she tries to observe, how the strokes improve on a daily basis, it will be almost impossible to do so. But once she continues doing it for a few months or years, we can easily notice the progression. Comparing her previous drawings to the recent ones and we know how much she has improved.

For children to draw is not difficult. All children are great artists, they just need a crayon and a wall. Any two year old can turn the whole house into a canvas. Moreover, they can show you many beautiful imaginative creatures just by scribbling and doodling on the walls of their house. But then this is where the direction changes. If we stop the children from messing around the house, we inhibit their growth. It is the easy scribbles on the walls that grow into carefully mastered strokes on canvas as your child grows.

What you should understand here is this. Making strokes on the walls can be your easy goals, which need little or no effort in doing. Also, you cannot measure them on a daily basis. We might not see any, or little, progress immediately. But if we continue doing them at a consistent rate, we slowly get better at it. They are a part of our natural progression towards mastery. It's only that they require very little but sustained and consistent effort.

There might be a plateau phase in your easy goals. There might be a time where you don't show any improvement in your tasks, where you don't produce effective results. When we tend to get focused on results that we think we should see daily, and when we don't see any improvements, it demotivates us. Emotionally, it becomes a very tiresome job to do. When we don't see immediate results, we can start to fixate on that one thing. When this happens, we get off our plan. We start trying to force things so we can get that little win and the adrenaline rush that goes with it. Like in my daughter's case, trying to learn drawing quickly by taking shortcuts will never work in the long term. It might even never help her. It might take her interest off drawing completely. This can be rather harmful, for her growth and learning. But this is where consistency and perseverance matters. Just by continuing to work on your easy goals, you can get out of this temporary plateau phase and continue to grow.

We can't always measure success of a goal by small, incremental steps. It's better to look at the larger scale of progress. A better question at these times is to see what pattern of improvement is appearing in her drawings? Is she improving on a larger scale, or is she getting stagnant and bored of her drawings? We need to see if we are trending downwards overall, starting to go back up or are we just where we are? This applies to all the goals that you set for yourself.

When slowing down, make sure that you see the larger picture and modify your approach based on those results. Be it drawing, or any goal in life, small or incremental goals, might not be visible at first, but they will slowly grow into massive results if we continue working on them on a consistent basis. The key is to never stop on the way to success. ❑

Chapter 5

Resolutions

Don't make resolutions without an action plan.
The secret to success is right in your hands.

–J. Allen Shaw

1. Achievers vs. Resolvers

It's that time of the year when we start making commitments to ourselves and to others about our New Year resolutions. These are goals that we decide to work upon for the rest of the year. Let me repeat, we wake up one fine day, and decide that for one whole year, we are going to get a major transformation happen in our life, by following some new year resolution. How is this possible, I must ask? For those who have made such resolutions, we all know, that a majority will give up on their resolutions, by the end of the first month. Few may even forget it by the coming week itself. An extreme example, the night owls, while partying on the New Year's Eve, might promise to themselves and to others that they need to turn into early risers. But they often forget their so called promise, as soon as the New Year party is over. The next day, all they wake up to is a nasty hangover, and a forgotten resolution. Let's call them Resolvers.

On the other side we have people, who take these resolutions very seriously, and for them the 1st of January is a magical time. This is the time where they make decisions to learn some new skills etc., and work upon it to turn it into a deeply ingrained habit. By making some serious commitments, they set their mental gaps to reach a certain destination, and press the start button. Then they work through the year, towards getting there. Slowly, their newly acquired bit turns into a habit, that start giving them better results as the year progresses. Let's call them Achievers.

So, the 1st of January is quite an important date for both the Achievers and the Resolvers. It is this time of the year when goals are either buried, or are begun.

Let's talk about the difference between these two groups. It begins with the attitude and mindset of both these groups, when they get started. The Resolvers, don't generally have a plan, or a date, or any specific goal that they decide to work upon. They just think of a certain resolution, that they should start working towards, and just announce it to the world. Grammatically, the definition of a resolution is 'A firm decision to do or not do something', but people end up making a joke out of it. It's about a whopping 99% of the people, who will forget all about their commitment by the end of January.

On the other hand, Achievers have a real plan and an innate desire to work towards their goal. It's their attitude that makes them commit to bring the desired change in their lives. They commit to themselves to keep working and trying, till they succeed in whatever endeavor they want to excel in. Moreover, it's not about just success, it is about their decision about doing what's necessary, and to stick to it throughout the year that makes the difference.

The other difference between the Achievers and the Resolvers is the way they have prepared to make changes. Achievers have a plan set for them. Even if it is not a specific plan, it still has a method to which they can adhere to on an everyday basis. The plan becomes the focus of their daily activities. They look forward to working on it every day, till it becomes second nature to them. The Resolvers on the other hand, have a very faint idea of how they are going to achieve their goal. Their plan usually lacks consistency. Due to this, they often come back to where they have started, and keep getting the results they have always been getting.

The similarity between them is that they both recognize that they want to change something in their lives. It's that they both are not satisfied with where they are, and they both are capable of identifying the point of change in their life. It's that both the Achievers, and the Resolvers, see what's hurting them, and decide to work upon bringing about the change that's needed to get rid of their pain. Achievers, know what hurts, and decide not to stay where they are. Yet, Resolvers, accept pain as their reality, and soon become comfortable with it and come back to their similar routine in a few days' time. For them, bringing the necessary change is not worth the amount of hard work or dedication it takes.

The basic difference is that of priorities. Even though both the groups know where to go, Achievers realize what's important, and decide to work towards it relentlessly. To give it what it takes, makes the difference between your resolutions being a success or a failure.

2. Keep Going with your New Year Resolutions

Why do people give up on their new year resolutions? Everyone who starts working on their resolutions start with a lot of passion and enthusiasm towards accomplishing their goal. If only this was enough, we would have achieved all that we had aspired for.

There may be a number of reasons behind people not sticking to their New Year resolutions. We need to understand a bit about this before we move any further.

The main reasons that stop ourselves from going ahead, in spite of having enough passion and enthusiasm towards our goal are due to lack of knowledge towards our behavioural change. We all know that any change, to be hardwired in our brain has to begin from the inside. This behavioural change to happen depends on the influence of the outside world as well.

There are a few key elements of behavioural change that influence the fulfilment of a New Year resolution.

The first one is that of our basic attitude towards the change. This happens from the inside. If we ourselves are not comfortable with the change, it might not happen at all.

For example, suppose you want to kick a habit, let's say smoking, its only possible if the change that you look forward to, happens through your own willpower. However hard may anyone else try, if you yourself are not willing to change the habit, nothing else will. It is your attitude that determines the success or failure of any habit.

Any intentions or goals are built on three important

elements that serve as the foundation of being successful at keeping resolutions.

The first one is your own attitude around a behavior. It depends on you on how you look at any habit, either good or bad, from your perspective. If for say, your attitude towards smoking is that of it being okay, or you may think of smoking as a style substance, then you may never give it up.

Secondly, it is the society's attitude around your behavior. People around you may help you make or break a habit. If good health isn't on your top priority list, and you're surrounded with smokers who themselves have tried quitting smoking but only to fail, then setting yourself up towards quitting smoking will be a difficult task.

Thirdly, it is your own belief in your own ability to succeed at achieving or acquiring a new behavior. For example, if you plan to quit smoking and prioritize good health and you believe in it, there is a good chance that you will be able to break the habit. You will then, surround yourself with people who don't smoke, avoid any so called triggers that might get you back in the habit. Soon, you will feel strong enough about quitting smoking, so setting yourself up towards it won't be a problem.

Having just an intention to achieve a goal is not enough. Just deciding to do it will never work. There is a need to act and take on the right kind of behavior so that your intentions will turn into a reality, because if not, then goals will never be achieved.

Once we understand this concept, acquiring a new behavior, and carrying on with it becomes easy.

3. Four Reasons you will fail in your resolutions

1: You don't have a strong "Why"

In order to complete your New Year resolutions you have to have a "why" behind it. Like mentioned earlier, a clear "why" is important to give you energy to keep going with your resolutions. If you have a weak attitude about reaching your goals, there is a major chance that you will never be able to accomplish it. Your resolution might be slightly difficult to keep up with in the beginning, but your "why" should be the reason to keep you going. Thinking of the larger picture, and the impact of what your New Year resolutions will have in the long term is what might get you towards achieving them. Say you make a resolution to save more money, it's better to have a clear reason behind it. It can be that of giving your children a good education in the future. The more close to your heart the reason is, the more likely you are to achieve it.

Thinking of some introspective questions can work towards identifying your Why. It can be something like, learning how to cook, so that you can help your wife in her daily chores. Or it can be something like learning a new language, so that you can communicate and apply for the new job that requires you to be proficient in that language.

A good reason of why you want something can work wonders for you even when you are feeling low and it will keep you motivated throughout your journey. Finding such causes will always help you be on the right track to achieve your resolutions

2: Having a poor support system

More than thinking about surrounding yourself with cool people, it's important that you have forged close connections to people who will hold you responsible for the accomplishment of your goals. Even the most successful person will sometimes struggle in finding the motivation and accountability to keep a New Year's resolution. That is why surrounding yourself with people who care enough about your success will help keep you focused.

Suppose you realize that you are weak in Physics and decide to score better marks in it. You decide giving it some extra time, and put in some extra effort to learn the chapters. While you are at it, your study is interrupted by a phone call from a cool friend who has planned to explore a new discotheque along with other close friends. Now I want you to sit and evaluate the probability of you sitting at home doing the physics lessons (in which you are already weak) or going out with your friends to the new discotheque and partying through the night.

Moreover if you are surrounded by a group of students who are good in the subject, and are always willing to help you solve your Physics problems, you are more likely to score better marks in the subject in the upcoming exam.

The same applies to sticking to your New Year resolutions. More than being surrounded by cool people, it's always better to have close connections who will help you work towards your goals. Such people help you stay focused, and keep you accountable for what you want to achieve.

It is said that the five people you spend most of the time with is who you most likely are or who you'll become. That's how important is the role of people you decide to spend time with plays in your life.

It's always good to find and surround yourself with such people. Again, your close connections can either help you or break you into keeping your goals. People who will challenge you, will hold you responsible, will always help you grow for the better.

3: Setting goals that are too easy or too difficult

Suppose you set a goal to run for 30 minutes, four times a week. For the athletic types, it is too easy a goal. The athlete, who is physically in a good form, will hardly ever feel pain in doing such a workout. At the same time, he won't show any considerable improvement also. What if he wants to prepare for an athletic meet? Do you think this kind of preparation is enough for him to train for the competition?

On the other hand, imagine an obese woman in her mid-40s, who decides to jog for the same time as the athlete. Will she be able to achieve the same goal with that ease? She might give up on the first day itself.

Self-efficacy, loosely defined, is a psychological belief that is related to one's ability to be successful in the accomplishment of one's goals.

There are two ways to judge if a person is capable of achieving his goal or not. One is that how confident the person is about his ability to complete a goal. If it's too easy a goal, one is bound to get bored, or might show little or no improvement in achieving it. Secondly, if it's too difficult a goal, one is sure to give up in between. It all depends on how likely a person will act upon the challenge he has set upon himself in order to complete the goal.

Goals need to be challenging, as well as achievable at the same time. It's better if achieving the goal makes you uncomfortable, while at the same time you know that you can do it if you put in some extra effort.

In the athlete's case, it's better to create a more challenging goal for himself, either by increasing the time, or the intensity of the workout. In the woman's case, it's better to break the goal into small bite size pieces so that she can keep going with her exercise routine, without getting bored or demotivated by it.

A better way of doing this is to find a mentor or a coach who can guide you through your goals. Also, listening to audiobooks, reading motivational books and watching such videos, will help you stay motivated in moving towards your goal.

4: Not taking enough Action

A major problem with taking action is that people avoid getting into situations they have never been in before, to avoid failure. At times, taking action needs people to get out of their comfort zone. That is why a proper action plan is required.

Also, a better thing to do is to work on your plan step by step. To break the larger goals into several easier steps, makes it easy for you to take action, and to mark your progress.

Small steps taken in the right direction, help you to progress towards your goal. Also, when done at a consistent basis, helps you gather momentum.

Taking action should not be optional. Make sure that you are doing something for your goal, even if it is a very small thing to do. For example, just a small phone call, or a message dropped to someone, can sometimes help you to add momentum towards your goal.

One thing you have to be careful is to not repeat similar actions, if things have not worked out correctly in your previous attempts. If you have not made any progress earlier, it's time for you to map a different route, and work towards it. Mapping out all the options, and choosing just one or two methods, and working upon them can help you get your job done. In some situations, thinking out of the box, or doing something unusual is often the right thing to do.

These four reasons when worked upon, will never let you fail at your resolutions. Keeping these four factors in mind, and working towards your goals, will give you guaranteed results which will be beyond what you can imagine.

4. The 5th Secret to Successful Resolutions

Are you amongst the ones who make New Year resolutions in January every year, and then forget about them by the time the month ends? Chances are, that most of you belong to this category of people. Even so, some of them don't even remember what resolutions they made. Then there are the ones who don't complete them, feel guilty about not doing anything about them, and then move on with their lives.

If you are amongst the special few who make resolutions, stick to them and complete them, you don't need to read any further.

For the rest of us, we need to know this: those resolutions, and any other goals you set for yourself along the way, are much more easily and successfully accomplished when you actually appreciate and enjoy the journey in completing it.

When we look at the people pursuing different goals, the recurring pattern that emerges, shows us the difference between the achievers and the non-achievers. The achievers are the one who seem to have enjoyed the whole process of seeking the goal. An extensive study of a number of different goals, such as getting healthier and improved study habits, showed that when people enjoyed the process required to achieve their goals, they stuck with it. Like for instance, people who have wanted to improve upon their health, show considerable improvement if they enjoy working out with their barbells and weights. Whereas when people, for example, exercised only for the sake of better health, but didn't enjoy lifting weights or running on the treadmill or whatever method they chose for their exercise, guess what? Within a few weeks' time, they have given up on their dream and are back to their previous self.

Coming to think on it, these are the people who feel guilty about it for some time, and then they go about their life like nothing ever happened. These are the few who remain the same throughout their life. Making New Year resolutions and not keeping up to them, becomes their habit, so much so that after a few times, they even stop feeling guilty about not accomplishing them.

The goal itself may be interesting enough, like to learn a new language, or to learn how to swim, or to drive a car. But for most of us, just by having a desired end in mind isn't enough to give you the persistence it takes to get there. You have to enjoy the process.

The best way to go about your New Year resolutions is to make the process more fun. You must choose how you plan to accomplish it while making it a fun process at the same time.

Like if you want to learn to swim, enrolling into a swimming club, with your partner, keeping each other accountable, hiring a good coach who pushes you towards learning and improving upon your technique in an encouraging way, is one of the few methods to make learning how to swim a fun activity.

See what suits you the best and go ahead with it. Soon you will be on the path of accomplishing your goal. So with a smile and a sense of confidence, you can begin your journey towards being a winner.

❑

Chapter 6

Values and Beliefs

"Values are like fingerprints. Nobodies are the same but you leave them all over everything you do."

–Elvis Presley

1. Your biggest goal may not be as important

What is your biggest goal? The biggest that you can think of. Now think of your most important goal. Are they the same? Your biggest goal may not be as important. Similarly, your most important goal may not be as big. There is a difference. They look similar, you might think. But they are not. To know the difference between the two, the best way is to think upon the difference. What makes a goal big? It can be the size of the goal, or it can be the effort needed to accomplish it. It can even be the cost of the goal, or it may mean the number of people who are going to benefit from it. Now when we think about the importance of the goal, the size becomes irrelevant. What matters is that what impact that goal will have on the people around it.

I would like to share an example of an important goal and a big goal to explain this. Suppose I plan to travel to outer space and mark it as my most important goal in life. I complete the necessary studies and excel in all my physics and mathematics subjects. I also score well in my physical education classes. I enter the college of my choice and pass with good marks in all the courses that I need to become an astronaut. Now, after working on it for many years, I finally become an astronaut and get to travel to outer space. Once back, I even get awarded for my endeavors.

Now, becoming an astronaut and flying into outer space, may be the most important goal in my life, but it is not as important in the eyes of others. It may be big enough for others to accomplish, but it does not help them in any special way. This makes the goal important and big for me, but since it is not as impactful for others, it may not be as important for them. It wouldn't matter much to them if I or someone else travelled to space.

For the second example:

Now you want to open a school for special children in your town. It may not be a big school. It might not involve a cost that you needed to become an astronaut or fly into outer space. But the impact that you will make on the future of those special children and their families will be astounding. The effort also may not be as much, when compared to that of travelling to outer space. Opening a school for special children is relatively easier than passing in all your exams and becoming an astrophysicist. This makes the goal important in a different way, irrespective of the cost or the number of people involved in it.

In general, we tend to assign importance to the bigger goals, but it doesn't mean it's our most important goal. Importance is more about the emotional attachment we have towards our goals and what we'll get out of them besides a sense of achievement. Now on a personal level, one of my most important goals is to make the best use of my creative thought process by drawing, sketching and by reading more books. This is done on a regular basis to stimulate the creative parts of my mind. It doesn't cost much, nor takes a lot of people or has major effect on the world. But it's important to me because drawing has always been one of my most loved things to do. I'm sure it will have a great effect on me, in the sense that it will make me more fulfilled and satisfied with my life. I getting better and better at drawing will also reflect on other aspects of my life.

The time and effort needed to do work towards a goal, slowly becomes your second nature when you start spending time upon it. The same happens when you develop new habits. The best that you can do is to set time aside to work on your goal and keep working till it turns into a habit.

The size of the goals are never as important. Working towards your goals, irrespective of the size, with utmost focus, so that you can see the impact it makes on others, is another way of looking at your goal. Keep working on it till its method becomes a part of your daily routine and watch the magic happen.

2. Do you know how to win?

When you pursue your goals, there are times when you might feel worn out and frazzled in life. To the frazzled person, that is you in this case, it becomes so tempting to cheat your way to success. Cheating always looks easier and better, when compared to sheer hard work. If you have ever felt like cheating in a task, I have some bad news for you.

Once you have decided to cheat, be sure that it is a bad deal. Whatever you may get through cheating, might give you a burst of adrenaline in the short run. It might give you fame also. You might become rich in one way or the other. But this victory is nothing but empty from within. So what if it's only 'you' who knows about it. You might manage to get away with it, but deep down, inside your heart, you know you have cheated. Your inner voice or your conscience knows this and will keep reminding you about it time and again.

Even if you try running away from it, the guilt always manages to catch up and the truth is that however big your victory may be, from the inside you are still a loser.

Cheating usually happens when you see someone else winning consistently, and are tempted to take the risk of self-sabotage in the greed to win. But the truth, here is, that whether you win or not, you will always remain a loser. The only way to get out of this trap is the hard way, and that is to train for what you need.

If you want something badly, the best way to get it is by making real efforts in getting it, and to pay the price that you need to achieve the goal. Even if you try hard and don't win, there is always a next chance. And knowing that you have given it your best without compromising on your principles and core values. That itself is a victory.

There is genuine winning, if you decide to stand by your core values, and don't cheat. Winning here doesn't matter, neither does the result count. What counts here is your genuine effort behind the goal. Living life in an honest way, and reaping the rewards nature has for you is one way of living. The other way is to cheat and get whatever you want, and live a life full of regret. The choice is yours.

3. Which goal to strive for first? Professional or Personal

While pursuing our goals we often wonder of what is easier to achieve, a personal or a professional goal? Both are equally important for our growth and achieving them both depend upon having certain attributes. We need to be committed, and dedicated to achieve both. We also need to have that innate desire to achieve them. There are characteristics like, confidence, perseverance, dedication etc. that we need to keep working with in order to get to our goals.

If you look at professional goals, the easiest way to evaluate its grade of success is by asking yourself a simple question. It is "what value are you providing?" For example, if you are a part of the team working on a certain project, you should know your role clearly and decide upon the value you are providing, in reference to that role itself. Suppose you are a designer, you have to decide on what value, are you providing to the clients in reference to your designs. If you are a sales guy, the value of your product is what matters more to the customer. Are you providing that value to the customer? Giving a proper demonstration, and explaining the qualities of the product you are selling, determines the value of the product in your customer's mind. This is what you must strive to achieve.

Basically, professional goals involves working with others on their goals and getting them closer to their success. If you are a head of your department, you have to work on what value are you providing to the teammates under you. Your job is to help your clients and your teammates succeed. The more you are able to get to this, the more successful will you be.

Now coming to personal goals, it depends on factors that you have to control. If it is something, like learning how to sing, or maybe starting a new business, you have to decide upon the outcome of the goals and work towards them. Personal goals are dependent on your commitment. This is not to say that you don't have to stay committed to achieving your professional goals.

Both, professional, as well as personal goals are equally challenging and have their own needs and attributes. While professional goals depend upon the success of others, personal goals are all about yourself. Both require equal amount of motivation and dedication to achieve them. Which of them is easier to achieve, it is on how you see it?

Simply put, professional goals result in the value you provide for others. It is determined by the success of others. Personal goals result in the value you have defined for yourself. It is all about you and your dedication towards it. The common factor in both is value. This is what you should decide, and work on it till to you get your answer.

4. Appreciating the wealthy and their wealth

Many of us feel that if we get enough money, we'll be happy. Also, once we have accumulated all the tangible stuff, we can sit back, relax and take it easy. But this is not always the case. We see a different scenario with people who get a lot of money too soon. If we get the money we want to, there is no guarantee that we will remain rich forever.

Studies have shown that lottery winners, more often than others, end up worse off, a few years after their big wins. Most of the time, the money goes away, sooner than it came. Also, when it comes to happiness, they are amongst the few unhappy ones, who become even unhappier after they have lost their fortune. They are often broke, or are often found waiting for their next lottery win. That is if they ever win again.

If you are in this state, and you come across any kind of a monetary gain, you might feel like you have got everything in this world. You might feel that all your problems have been taken care of and you are out of trouble forever. But it is seldom true. Sooner than you think, your money will disappear, in the same way it came to you.

Do you know where it will go? To the rich. Yes, it will go back to the wealthy people, from where it came from. It's usually said that if you take all the money in the world and spread it out evenly, the rich would get it all back in ten or twenty years.

Now if this ever may happen, you might think as the rich to be greedy and manipulative. You might think of them to be the ones who have robbed you of your wealth. This approach as you must realize is not the right thing to have.

If we think of the rich to be evil, there is a rare chance that you will be rich yourself. It is all about the mindset that you have. Cultivating a poverty-based mindset, where we are jealous and afraid of the rich, can never make us wealthy. After all, if you truly do believe that having wealth, and the people that are good at making money are evil, how will you ever get a lot of it? Unless you believe that you are evil as well.

Also, if you appreciate what you have, you begin to value it more, thus making it easier for you to receive more. Having financial goals, and being successful achieving them, is solely based on the mindset you have cultivated within yourself. If you have a poverty-based mindset, you are bound to stay where you are.

The only way is to be grateful of what you have, and not think of wealthy people as evil and manipulative. Learn about wealth creation from the wealthy, and soon you will find yourself amongst them.

❑

Chapter 7

Spirituality

"The two most important days in life are the day you born and the day you discover the reason why."
– Mark Twain

1. Is it enough to have willpower?

These days I'm spending a lot of my time listening to audiobooks using an app I subscribed to a few months back. Whenever I surf through the short story section, I often come across success stories of various achievers and tycoons. These men and women are both experts in their fields and have had many inspiring stories backing their journey.

One common thing that occurs in all of these stories is that almost everyone, yes everyone started out small. Slowly they went through their life's struggles, went through a lots of hard ships and sufferings and came out as a new avatar of themselves.

Listening to such audiobooks often makes us think of the suffering of all such inspiring people. We also start relating the amount of suffering to the amount of success. It is very commonly understood by all this, is that more the misery, more is the appreciation for success? But does that mean that suffering is an integral part of the journey to success?

No, it may not be suffering alone, it can be boredom also. You might go through discomfort and sacrifice on your way to success. But an overall journey should have excitement and fun as well.

If we compare the amount of fun and excitement with the amount of boredom and struggle of the achiever, we will notice that the excitement part is a tad more than the boredom part in almost all the cases. This alone is enough for keeping the passion alive. The more passionate the person is towards his goal; the more is his level of excitement when compared to his amount of struggle. If at all, it is the other way around, perseverance kicks in and gives that another much needed boost of energy needed to reach the final destination.

Please think about it, would you continue to suffer today, in order to achieve a better future tomorrow? It's like students attending boring lectures in college, in classes they hate so they can get a degree in a field of work they think they'll love.

It's like you going to work every day and not taking interest in any of the activities that happen there. It's like spending your days behind your desk, looking at the clock every half an hour, and waiting for the day to get over. Then repeating this day after day for the next few years.

Some people do this with despair, while the few special ones attend the same lecture with full concentration and attention, however boring it may seem to be.

There are people in the same office, doing the same mundane task as the others, but they do it with interest and enthusiasm. They are packed with energy and they look forward to doing the same work the next day, and they even strive to do more along with it.

Punishing yourself today for a happy fulfilling life tomorrow is never a wise thing to do. It's better to take charge of your life and to rise above this level of suffering. The only factor that carries us above these boring and unpleasant periods in our job is that of passion and enthusiasm. It is this passion and enthusiasm that helps us find the fun stuff in our jobs. Passion and the inevitable consistency that flows from it is far more important to success than willpower. But it should be interesting and fulfilling and fun along the way.

Think about the goals you're working on. Do you feel passionate and enthusiastic about each step? If not, maybe you are working upon the wrong goals. You might need to tweak them a bit to make them more of a fun activity. Suffering towards achieving your goal is not a viable option. You need not do it every time during your pursuit. Yes, it will be exciting when you achieve them, but don't forget to enjoy it while you are getting at it.

2. Using your inner voice to achieve more

Well, with what we have spoken about till now, we clearly know that in order to achieve what we strive for, we need to take action on it. The actions we take are based on two driving forces. They can be either due to avoiding pain or to pursuing pleasure. Now, if what we do is causing us more pain than pleasure, we will clearly avoid it. This usually happens when we pursue long term goals. The small bouts of pain that we suffer on the way leads us to deviate from a path and we soon give up our pursuit. This is why most people don't do the things that are needed to succeed.

Now, the unfortunate part is that when we avoid pain, we kind of avoid the pleasure associated with achieving the goal. Soon we find ourselves guilt ridden, and even in more pain. This pain leads us to stagnate, and stagnation is not good.

There are only two paths for one to take, if one stagnates. Either upwards, or downwards. When we avoid taking action, we have unconsciously, shut the door that will take us upwards. Now what is left is the path that will lead you to decline.

Another thing that stops us from moving forward, even before the pain strikes in is the 'fear' of pain. If our mind tries to stop us from moving forward, it creates a sense of fear that stops us from doing what we ought to do. If we do not understand this and let mind play games with us, we are surely going to fall victim to this.

Now that we have understood the fact that it is our own mind that stops us from success, we can easily overcome this phase and come out of this situation.

One such strategy is to listen to your inner voice. "What inner voice? I don't have an inner voice!" you may ask. This is your inner voice. This is the voice in your head that does all the talking. It is always ready to give you advice and it hardly ever stops.

This is your subconscious mind speaking to you. Think of your subconscious mind as a giant store room with boxes lined up across the walls. Each box contains a memory associated with an incident in life. They are also stacked and labelled according to your age and experience. Let's assume that you had slipped from your bicycle, and fractured your ankle when you were ten years old. Now every time you try teaching your son to ride a bicycle, your subconscious mind simply slides that box containing that "my-slipping-off-the-bicycle" memory into your conscious mind and you start to remember that incident in detail. This memory makes you scared even before your son gets on the bike. How will you teach him, if you always think of your son falling off the bike?

This is what the subconscious mind does every time. Different negative events have happened to all of us that shape our decision-making as we get older. In this case, it might hamper your sons learning period.

Another example can be a type of food that reminds you of someone. My father, who is no more, was very fond of mangoes. Every time I see those certain type of mangoes, I almost every time think of him, and the fondness he had for the fruit. While, this piece of memory is very unique to me, it may not apply to anyone else. Seeing the same fruit, might not trigger a similar response in the mind of someone who does not like mangoes. It's the subconscious mind that connects different objects to different incidents or people, which might not be as relevant to anyone else. The point here is that your conscious mind refers to such boxes that are slid down by your subconscious mind. This majorly affects your thought process and your performance in different tasks that you take over. If the thought boxes are positive, or neutral, it does not matter. The negative advice coming from your subconscious is what we should try to control.

You see, most people do not understand the difference between subconscious and conscious thinking. It is the subconscious that can only make you successful if you work at conditioning it in the right way. There are times where we need to silence the chatter of our subconscious and need to focus it in the right direction. If you are willing to take responsibility for what your subconscious tells your conscious mind, the rest becomes easy. But it's not that simple, it needs real hard work.

There are a few ways in which you can control how your subconscious mind works. The best way is to overcome fear. Fear is an emotion, created in your mind that is just meant to protect you from any mishaps. But in most cases, it stops you from moving forward with your task. Every time, you have this feeling of fear stopping you from moving towards your goal, just try being aware of fear just being an emotion and nothing else. With practice, you will be able to overcome its negativity, and will learn to celebrate it. The more you do this, the more positive messages your subconscious will give your conscious when you come face to face with fear. Once you pass over this mental hurdle, you literally become unstoppable.

Another way to get friendly with your subconscious mind, is through exercise. I used a very unusual method to work on my subconscious mind when I used to do cycling. There were times when I used to feel a little lazy, but would convince myself to take a small round on my bike and come back. As soon as I was on my bike, I used to start pushing myself a little. When my subconscious mind reminded that I was feeling tired, I would use my conscious mind to silence it, and decide to cycle a little further. As I would repeat the process, slowly adrenaline would set in, and I would forget all about being lazy. I usually ended up finishing a good workout with a heart full of satisfaction. Doing this, often helped me to choose between what my conscious mind and my subconscious mind had to say to me. I often use this method in other aspects of my life as well. It helps me to give my best, and I often go (again a pun) an extra mile at work also.

Meditation is also an effective method for silencing the subconscious mind. Giving yourself 20 minutes in the day, with no distractions around you can bring tremendous improvement in both your physical and mental health. Meditation, when done is even more challenging than exercising your physical body. It is more about silencing the mind. Many books and guided meditation courses are available these days to teach you how to do it. To silence the racing mind, and to condition it so that it helps you focus on the right things is a huge takeaway from meditation. By getting rid of the unwanted chatter, it also helps you to calm yourself. Different types of mediation techniques need to be practiced and experienced, as a foundation. You can choose what suits you the best and work towards making the best of it.

Another effective method of exercising your subconscious mind is that of using affirmations and declarations. Positive affirmations are the best content that you can feed your subconscious mind with. One of my dear friends Subrat Chowdhary, had a very interesting analogy to share with me about the subconscious mind. He compares the subconscious mind to be a wild hog. The interesting characteristic about this wild hog is that it is always hungry. It keeps on gobbling food. Now this hog does not know what the right food for it to eat is. It just knows, that it is hungry, and continues eating whatever comes its way. Now it is up to us to decide what we want to give our subconscious mind to eat. It can be negative thoughts, gossip, or whatever unhealthy thoughts you want to feed your brain with. Or it can be positive, healthy thoughts that will add to the efficiency of your subconscious mind.

When we use positive affirmations and declarations to feed our subconscious mind, we help our mind focus and grow on what's needed. When you decide to work on a goal, and feed yourself positive thoughts throughout the day, there are more chances for you to accomplish them. You also carry that positive disposition with you, throughout the day, as an added benefit. Usually writing out certain declarations on paper, and then saying them aloud in front of the mirror every morning is an effective way to feed your subconscious mind with some good and healthy food. This simple technique, then keeps your subconscious mind in check so that it gives right instructions to the conscious mind when needed.

A rather interesting method is to work on your self-development. Filling your mind with the right kind of knowledge is the best thing you can do. I often spend time reading the right kind of books, and by educating myself upon the topics that I need to work upon. Also listening to audiobooks as I drive on my way to work, is another different way of feeding my brain with the right kind of information. Avoiding silly soaps, and trash news is also as important. Using them for entertainment is good, but to use them to kill your time, or to fill your mind with trash, is a strict no-no.

To be inspired, and to fill your wild hog with the right kind of food is what you should continue working upon. It is a process that we need to learn to put ourselves on the path to success.

3. Are you still not getting what you want?

How much does your dream mean to you? Are you ready to give to the necessary time and effort to see it accomplished? If you want to achieve something, you have to believe in the possibilities of you achieving it. If you yourself don't trust in your abilities, no one else will.

You have to put in a lot of effort, or even reach out to any extreme for your dreams. You might have to tread on uncomfortable paths, or you might have to make your own path towards your destination.

You have to face every challenge that comes your way, improving and correcting your approach as you progress ahead. This could amount to a lot of time and hard work but you must be willing to put in that hard work whenever needed.

Also, don't think of your dream as only yours. It is a dream of everyone who supports you and helps you get on with the goal. Then it also becomes your responsibility to not let down those people who stand by you during your tough times. Even though you and your effort may not be as significant to the rest of the world, these are the people to whom each of your actions matter a lot. It is for them that you have to keep going on.

It happens sometimes that my set designs get rejected and I have lost a few work projects due to various reasons. But that does not mean that I get disheartened and depressed and stop working. In such situations, giving the best is the most we can do.

We must remember that no one is perfect in this world. We need to keep going and keep moving. Nothing is perfect except the ways of the Higher Power. Trusting in this power and working and improving along the way should be our ultimate goal.

Success comes to people who don't stop. It is not like winning a lottery, and getting an instant cash prize. It is more like building something bit by bit, step by step. No matter what obstacles surge, each person must continue to work on it. There are no shortcuts to success. These small attempts of trying to accomplish a purpose are already a part of your larger success. These small victories are the ones that transform into big goals with time.

You should keep reminding yourself that there is never a shortcut to success. It is always through hard work. This hard work, when put in the right direction, along with the support and love of the people who trust in you transform your life. This is the power that changes your future towards a brighter tomorrow.

With every obstacle that you cross, you should not just learn from it, you should also learn to trust the Higher Power. This should also be accompanied with a sense of gratitude towards the Higher Power and your well-wishers.

It is during these times that you will realize the true values of the people who value you the most. This is your ray of hope. This is your power. This is your courage.

In the worst of times, you will understand the profundity of life and purpose.

Along the way, you will see small wins and the larger victory. So, work on your attitude, encourage yourself… And get going.

4. You, a tiny speck in the Universe

There are days where nothing happens the way it's meant to be. Everything goes wrong. We find ourselves surrounded with situations and people against us. We feel stuck in the circumstance, trying hard to keep things going. This is a very sad situation where we feel that the whole world is against us.

Now imagine yourself as a tiny speck of being within a large substance, say a sphere. You as a speck may feel that the sphere, or the outside world is against you, the tiny speck of being.

In this state of mind, you might start imagining different scenarios of how the things will go wrong. How will everyone react against you and how the universe will conspire against you, stopping things from happening the way you want it to be?

Then there are people who leave such things to the Higher Power. Instead of getting drained by negative thoughts, they imagine themselves to be a part of the larger sphere, and learn to adapt and modify their plan accordingly. Though, they still are a speck, they feel as though the big sphere is a part of them and on the whole, have an intention of loving what they do. They treat all as one and feel everything that is happening is for the good and is a part of life.

This here is a choice, either to feel overwhelmed, or to make a decision and accept things as they are and take decision of setting things right, in the given situation. They then focus on what they as a speck can change and focus upon that only.

They choose to concentrate on their Now, which is what they have full knowledge of. And they work within what they can influence in their Now. Presence gives them the ability to control their mental state. They chose to put all their attention to their here and now. Just because they do this, they are aware of their emotions and thoughts.

If you choose to be in the now, you will soon be living free of all the clutter and disturbances that the mind imagines. Being in the here and now will give you an opportunity to live in the moment and face things the way the things are and not in the way you have imagined them to be.

Whatever comes up then, will not be laden with unnecessary thoughts and emotions, but will be made of well-structured thoughts and feelings. Now you won't have to throw your mind here and there, imagining some rubbish, but you will only imagine something that is congruent to your inner peace and desire.

Once you have been through this, you realize that the universe and its stress upon you is not personal, and that it is made of self-created illusions. It's just that what we have not understood, we deem it as wrong. It is not so. Walking on this planet with a head full of worries, will not make things better for you. You trying to control everything that is out of your reach will bring you unnecessary tension and trouble. There are more things relating to your life than you are aware of at this level of your existence. You are thus held hostage by your own personal plans.

Remember that your life always creates the next moment of your experience out of your intentions. Whatever you give attention to grows. So, what is the point of your mind at this level, concerning planning? Well, it is to execute the plans it receives, knowing with certainty that it cannot fail. You have to become a certain person for certain things to flow through you. It is this that you can use your lower mind for, by following cues from the higher mind. You form a vibration that matches what you desire. The attainment of success is not something that one comes by through chasing after success – it is something one attracts by the person they become. It is an inner journey of transformation. You can call it education, training, skills, self-help, discipline... it is all an inner transformational journey resulting in a frequency match. The rest has already been taken care of earlier. It is guaranteed. That is all you have to do.

It is fine to trust your personal plans when things start to go wrong. It is very natural to do so. After all it's your only choice. It is the only thing that you can use to try getting out of any unworthy situation. But then comes a time when this personal plan of yours starts to become a problem for you. It's your plan that now starts to interfere with your progress. This is the time to let it go. It is this moment when you have to let go of your fixated thought process and look forward to other options. Try looking at other plans, various plans. This is the time to let go of all your previous supports and trust in the higher being. It's time to give the Higher Power a chance and trust in it.

See what happens. Do it a few times, and listen to the

things and signs as they come and prepare yourself to see what comes by. No need to carry your previous emotional baggage on your head. Drop the load and start moving. Start trusting in yourself and the larger sphere. Remember, you are a tiny speck with a limited amount of thought. The universe is a larger, much larger entity, which moves by itself. It does not depend on you. It has its own collective thought process; it has its own rules. You are here to be in it and to trust the process.

If you are a part of the universe, and a part of the collective thought process it holds, how could you go wrong? This feeling itself is very liberating. It will help you trust yourself during times of adversity. Try doing it and you will start to trust it. Just by trusting it will make you free of all your mental burdens. Just be a part of the larger sphere. Try it.

❑

Chapter 8

Law of Attraction

Whether you think you can or think you can't, either way you are right.
– Henry Ford

1. In Law of Attraction, this is what you should know…

For most of us, thinking about the Law of Attraction might seem like a complicated jargon with lots of equations to solve. Or it may seem like an out of world experience that needs lot of time and concentration.

Let me tell you something. It is neither. Neither is it as complicated, like we may imagine it to be, nor is it as time taking or strenuous. Had it been as strenuous or tedious, it wouldn't have been accepted as a concept by us. The bottom line of human psychology is this, the more difficult the process is, the more we are less likely to accept it.

If visualization or believing in Law of Attraction was full of complicated imagery and difficult mental sequences, we would never have accepted it as something possible. It would always be considered as magic or unreal.

For example, if the secret to achieving an unlimited life of wealth and success, was to imagine some complicated visualization full of complicated calculation and tedious mental work, we'd all be broke forever.

Something like the Law of Attraction is powerful because of it being not so complicated. It being a simple process is the reason it becomes so acceptable.

Basically, Law of Attraction consists of two parts.

The first part is to decide upon the "element" that you want to manifest in your life. Then, whatever it is, you have to imagine it as clearly in your mind by giving it proper shape, size, texture, and feelings. The picture of you owning or possessing it should be as clear and vivid as possible.

Second, you have to live the feeling with as many positive emotions as you can. This becomes the essence of effective Law of Attraction.

By simply doing this, you will get the thing that you want to attract from the Universe.

But, what is "the Universe"?

Suppose you were the only person in this world, living in a beautiful house next to the beach, having some delicious food to eat, enjoying all the comforts of life. Also you have time for yourself each evening to watch the beautiful sunset.

Strolling along the beach is fine, watching the beautiful sunset is also fine, and you may not need anyone else for that. But somewhere, it might be trouble for you to live in a beautiful house because you would have to get it constructed first. Getting delicious food for yourself also might need someone to get it on the table for you. Do you think it is possible for you to be the only person existing in this world? The simple answer is no. Enjoying any luxury in life, apart from the ones nature has given, is possible only if someone apart from yourself, helps you.

So the universe here, where you want to enjoy the luxuries of life only comes through the help and cooperation of only one element.

Other People!

However hard you may try, Law of Attraction will not work effectively till other people are involved. Also, it does not mean being surrounded by people and by wishing they too guess what you want, then praying that once they have guessed it, they will move ahead to help you achieve it.

Law of Attraction works through interacting and associating with other people. However, vivid and clear your imagination may be, about the thing that you want to achieve, however strong may be your emotions, you will not be able to achieve even one of your desires and goals, till you associate and interact with the other people. This is your Universe.

Just thinking about your desires and adding emotions to it, is a part of the process. But it's incomplete.

Now you know what completes it.

2. Destiny vs. Law of Attraction

This by far will be the most difficult chapter for someone to comprehend. Here I have tried to relate Law of Attraction in a spiritual context. Reading it carefully and trying to understand what I will be explaining here, will be a revelation point in the reader's mind.

Now let's look at the spiritual context of Law of Attraction. For some, attaining something might not be materialistic. It might be something related to the mind or the self. Some might even be searching for peace of mind, or tranquility etc.

Let us give it a common name, let's call it the search of truth.

Now anything related to search, materializes in two ways. Either it manifests through Law of Attraction or you are driven towards it through the power of destiny.

Both these concepts are valid enough. But at the same time they are contradictory.

Now if you want to search for something that is not coming to you so easily, the first thing you will need to do for either Law of Attraction or destiny to work for you is that you will have to drop all your existing opinions.

You will have to get over your current state of mind.

Searching for the truth.

Getting rid of fixed opinions in your mind requires you to do two things. First is to believe in the ultimate truth, however incomprehensible it may be. Had it been easy to believe, it wouldn't have required faith to do so. Secondly, it requires one to rise above the present mental state and avoid being carried away with previous experiences. Taking references from previous experiences and sticking to them will not let you absorb the new concept. You might get to understand a part of the ultimate truth, but it will remain biased, making it impossible to attain.

Once we break through our challenging opinions, and rise above our current state of mind can we understand the concept of receiving something in outer life? Now receiving something new in our life comes through these two contradictory principles, the Law of Attraction and or Destiny.

If you are already in possession of a few objects that you had ever desired to possess, it would have been due to these two reasons only. It is your perspective that decides, the method that you believe in.

Now, the Law of Attraction requires one to imagine, emote and live in that state of mind, believing into attaining what you want. This in turn manifests itself and you finally attain it.

Destiny on the other hand, means that however hard you may try, Law of Attraction will not work for you if it's not meant to be. What will happen will happen, and it has nothing to do with you trying to attract something in your life.

If you believe in both these concepts, you are living in a state of contradiction. If not on the physical level, but on a deeper level, it will always make you indecisive. If you remain indecisive for a long time, one thing will clearly happen. That you will end up nowhere. Then this stagnant situation of yours will become your destiny.

So developing a connection with Law of Attraction and destiny becomes utmost important if you want things to change in your life.

Destiny is an excuse of not using Law of Attraction in your life. It is basically a phase where you are ready to accept things as they are, and not trying to change for the better. It is also an excuse of not trying harder and living in fear. It is an excuse where you decide to live with your fixed opinions and stop accepting anything new in your life. This is where one gets comfortable in accepting what one is getting in this life and lives in denial for any other parallel life to exist. Basically, he lives in denial of a better life.

To live in denial, and not working on things to change is an extremely sad state to be in. We need to accept the following principles to get out of this situation.

Firstly we need to believe in both the principles but with a change in perspective.

Law of Attraction works in making things happen. But only if you believe in it, and live with it in a reasonable and workable manner. You cannot just lie on your bed and dream of attaining a million dollars. Chances of attaining a million dollars will be not even one in a million (Pun intended) for the Law of Attraction to work. It is necessary for you to work towards it. In fact, Law of Attraction helps you to introspect upon your need and your inner conscience guides you find a path to achieve it. Only thing that you need to get rid of here is your fixed opinions.

Destiny on the other hand gets you the chances to attain your goals. It is an expert in delivering opportunities. If you believe in Law of Attraction, you will be able to identify these opportunities and will find ways of making it fruitful. If not, they will simply drift away, and your present situation will become your destiny.

If you want things to change, you will have to use your power to choose between the right and the wrong opportunity.

To choose between opportunities, that destiny gives you, you always have to remember this. Never decide based on someone else's opinion who is benefitting by your loss. It should always be your opinion, based on what you have imagined for yourself, again based on your methods.

Both Law of Attraction and destiny, however contradictory statements, they may be, will work in your favor, if you learn to see them in the correct perspective.

3. The Body Language of Success

Have you ever checked your posture? Or anyone's posture by that way. It's not about keeping shoulders back, or spine erect, or keeping the chin up. It's about the posture that influential, confident, successful people have. It's about having a posture of a trustworthy, confident and an "I-know-what-I-do" person.

In the business world, being successful and having a correct posture is very much related to each other. It is our body language that the person in front of us observes and captures, without us even being aware of it. Also, it's our posture, and our body language that makes people rely on us and believe in what we believe in.

Where we stand in life, also depends on the aura we carry with us. A great analogy to this is that of a finishing line of a race. Imagine that you have just finished a two hundred meters sprint and have just crossed the finish line at the third position. Now you stand on the podium with two other fellow runners to receive the medal.

Now, you can relate this third position of yours to where you are now in life. This step where you are is your present situation in the various roles that you play in life. It can be your career, your family, business or health.

The person who is at the second position, is at the next level of success, in the same regions that you are. It is just the same, only that he is at the next level of your business, life or health. That is the next step that you need to achieve.

Similarly, the person who stood first is at the pinnacle of his position in life, business, and health etc. This comes as a result of the player giving his best performance, that's even better than all the other participants.

Now, the struggle here is to reach at the next level, and then become the best person that you want to be. Suppose I'm at third position as an Art Director, it becomes imperative for me to bring about certain improvements in my way of living and working, to get me to the next level of success.

For this I need to have clarity of what all do I need to do in order to raise my level up by one step. Then the better I do, the better I get. This if continued, will get me to the top level of whatever I want to achieve.

If I relate it to my profession and consider myself at level three, I might think of something like this. "I am a successful art director because of my ability of creating beautiful designs, keeping the clients happy and satisfied, while taking great care of my employees as well." These attributes, and a few more have got me to this level in my career so far. If I want to move a level up, I may have to think and plan on accomplishing more at the workplace, being more proactive, being more approachable, etc. I would simply look ahead of me keeping in mind the qualities and attributes that I need to build in me to get to the next level. Likewise, the same applies to me if I want to reach the top.

Then comes the magical revelation. Come to think of it, the body language of the people on these three levels are markedly different than each other. It's just that we have to be observant enough to notice this. Most of the work required to climb from one level to the next one is internal. It happens on the inside. It happens because of the change in our body language. That comes from a compilation of diligent action, accumulated experiences, client satisfaction, positive core values, etc. The advancement up the scale of success is highly influenced by the belief we have in ourselves.

Very often small business owners and new comers undervalue themselves. They seem to be less confident about their work, their products and their pricing. As a result, sell themselves too short. My brother who is an expert in sales often tells me that every customer has his own price point. One just has to create a product to match it. This is such a fine example of someone wanting to create something that will take him/her to the next level.

It's all in the mind. It's only a matter of a mind shift. It's only about changing one's perspective and looking at things from a different angle.

It is not about you being better than others, or that others are not as good as you are. It's just a mental shift. It's just about you being aware of what you need to do to get to the next level and to continue doing it with humbleness and integrity. It is just about keeping your eyes on the goal of becoming a master in whatever field that you want to be, and continue doing it till you reach a level up, and ultimately become an expert in whatever you want to be. It is just about moving towards your goal and being world class.

It is now time for you to take responsibility of your actions, and move ahead with the air of confidence and fearlessness. You don't have to justify your actions to yourself. You just have to keep moving. You just have to keep working on your body language, till you reach to the next level and become a master in your field. So, start running my friend, not for a third place, but for the first. Run, win and then celebrate. Carry yourself like a winner, and you surely will win.

4. Why did Law of Attraction stop working?

Let's imagine that you have set every factor concerned with achieving your goal in place. You have decided on a clear goal in mind. You also have painted a vivid picture of it and have been able to make a plan on how to achieve it. You also have a burning desire in your heart to achieve it. In other words, your "why" is also clear. In fact, the better you have imagined it, the better are the chances of you to achieve it. You have given it your time and energy, and have started to take the necessary action also. Now all you need to wait for is your goal to manifest. It is then, that things start to get difficult.

Sometimes achieving a goal becomes impossible, many times due to reasons we are unaware of. There are times where we are on our quest to achieve our goal, and we know that everything we had in out or plan is working fine.

In this case, while everything you might have thought of is in the right place, something suddenly brings your plans to a halt. You check and crosscheck each parameter. You try looking into your plan and wonder what went wrong? Maybe you are in a place where Law of Attraction has always worked for you. Your self-esteem is high due to previous less-sized victories, and you are full of energy to venture into your next quest. This is your new, grander vision of what you want for yourself.

In spite of your immense self-confidence and positivity due to your past victories, there is this thing happening, which will lead you to failure. Worse, it can strangely sap you out of your energy and can demotivate you. This can happen despite you knowing that you are capable of success.

Have you wondered what can be wrong? What is behind all this that its happening?

Well this time it's not any external object that has come your way. It is your own dear Self-worth.

It could be an inner belief that we are not worthy of that degree of accomplishing our goal. Due to this, we might lower the level of our goal. We might even convince ourselves to settle for less. We may even take steps to reduce the intensity of our mission. It might be our lack of belief in ourselves that may convince us that we do not deserve the level of success that we have visualized for ourselves. Once this feeling sets in, it becomes almost impossible for us to win. This can continue happening in other areas of our life, if left unresolved.

You may wonder if it has happened to you before. Also, if have you have had this feeling earlier?

(Perhaps, it may have come from our conditioning during childhood. It could have been from parental attitudes or a reaction to a particular experience. However, we are far more likely to succeed in that if we try to go back in our minds to find the origin for this lack of belief in what we deserve. Some mental blocks stay in our mind much longer than we can ever imagine. To identify them and to get rid of them is the only way to succeed.)

It may have been possible, that you might not have been through such a challenge before. Or maybe that your earlier challenges have been too easy for you. With success coming easily to you, it's understood, that you may feel exasperated and frazzled, when going through such a situation.

"Is there a way out of this?"

Of course, there is a way out, and the best way is to question your belief system. We need then to ask ourselves whether any one of these beliefs is something we want to continue to live by. Or should we restructure our thoughts so that they become our guiding force instead of pulling us back?

Such questions, when asked to oneself, will help us identify our mental block. It's all about our hard work and perseverance in the right direction. If we feel we are happy in our heart, while doing the task, we must also realize that the success that we are looking for is a much deserved thing. That we deserve every bit of success attached to the task, and it has nothing to do anything with our being less skilled or incapability. Victory is what we should always strive for, and live for. Not being worthy enough, is simply out of the question.

❑

Chapter 9

What if you fail?

"Failure should be our teacher, not our undertaker. Failure is delay, not defeat. It is a temporary detour, not a dead end. Failure is something we can avoid only by saying nothing, doing nothing, and being nothing."

– Denis Waitley

1. Why is it taking so much time?

Are you amongst the few people who often get frustrated when things don't happen the way you have wanted them to? Do you ever get frustrated wondering why it's taking so long for you to achieve your goals and manifest your abundance? Well, here's some news for you. You are a part of a very big lot that thinks the same.

A lot of people have such worries and it takes a big part of their day. They often worry that the things that they have so badly wanted to achieve, will never be theirs. Simply speaking, they will never get what they long for.

Such thoughts also occur when what these people have wanted gets delayed due to some reason.

Thoughts like, "I will never get it", I should try for something else", and "It will never happen," are a few examples of such thoughts. The above thoughts are partly because our society is very action-based. These negative thoughts often get multiplied many times over.

Now if things are not happening your way, you can look at it a bit differently for a while. There can be a number of reasons, why things are not happening according to your expectations.

If you have heard about the Law of Gestation, you will know that anything that you have done is like planting a seed. It takes time to grow and flourish. Maybe you are not giving your 100% towards your actions to bear fruit. Give it some time to flourish. Nurture your aspirations with some meaningful actions and let them grow into a beautiful crop. Give it time.

Maybe you are working hard on solving a problem, but you are not doing the right thing. Taking right action will get you the right result. Remember, everything that you do is a combination of cause and effect, action and reaction. Only doing the right action will get you the desired results.

Secondly, maybe you are taking the right actions, you are even covering the entire process that's needed to get what you want, but deep down you are not trusting the process. Somewhere inside, you know that you are not going to get it. This is where the Law of Attraction comes in. If you believe, even if subtly, that you will not get anything, there's some news for you. You won't. Your own subconscious mind is keeping the desired thing from coming into your life.

If you act in one way, and think in the opposite way, how do you expect things to happen smoothly?

Some examples of doing the things and wishing for the opposite is that of wanting to earn more money. You might wish for a higher salary, or even work hard towards acquiring wealth, but at the same time you worry that if you earn more, people will start calling you selfish. Or that you will get surrounded by people who will steal or rob you of your money. Such kinds of thoughts will never get you rich.

Similarly, if you dream of owning a large business and you worry about how you would handle every aspect of it, once it starts to happen. This is a guaranteed path to failure and you are bound to lose on the way.

These are examples of the few mental blocks that people carry with them throughout their life. Such blocks can be related to any aspect of your life, be it health, money or business. They are often a result of childhood conditioning. It is rather unfortunate that such thoughts come to us from our parents and close ones and are often fed to us throughout our lives. Such blocks have to be taken care of ASAP and the sooner you get over with this, the better it is.

Lastly, once you have been through all this negative thought process, your own self-image changes. You start to believe that you don't deserve it. That's because of the story that you've been telling yourself for so long of who you are and what you've gotten really good at and so on. For example, if you always see yourself as a struggling entrepreneur, it may be difficult to see yourself as a successful businessman. You can't imagine what it would be like to easily pay your bills on time.

Also, let's not forget that such occurrences often result in a lot of desperation. Once you start to doubt your self-image, you might even get desperate behind something. This leads to unwanted stress and it's pretty difficult to attract great, cool stuff (money, clients, opportunities, and so on) when you're stressed out. At that point, you're repelling the abundance away.

A better way of dealing with it is to get rid of old stories and conditioning. Practice manifesting to strengthen that manifestation muscle. If needed, get support to get rid of negative beliefs, negative thoughts, worries, and fears so you can move forward. Then, putting together a strategy and realistic timeline should work. Continue to take consistent action.

Remember, the Universe or the Higher Power, or whatever you may call it, is here for you. It will get you what you want.

2. Past disappointments? What to keep and what to forgo?

I happened to lose a major work contract a few years back. Though we had spent many years in designing sets for movies; television and award shows were relatively new to us. We had just started my art direction company then, and not many people knew about us. We were still waiting for our major breakthrough. Then one day this opportunity came and we readily grabbed it. It was a set of an award show for which we soon prepared a beautiful, functional and intricate design. I and my team had poured in days of hard work behind the design of the set. In fact, everyone was very excited for the project to begin. We were very confident that we had created a very beautiful design, and it was bound to get approved. While we impatiently waited, for the design to get approved, the unwanted happened.

We got to know the result early the next afternoon. The set had been given to another art director. Though, the client and other decision makers had liked our design and had loved the overall functionality and the aesthetic balance of the set, they decided to go for another art director, telling us that they were not ready to bank upon some newcomers. This reply came as a shock to us and for a while me and my team was very uncomfortable about the whole thing.

It's been years since then, and we have quite successfully constructed many elegant and beautiful sets for various award shows. But the incident of that lost project was quite an experience for us.

This happens many times with new comers. However talented and efficient one may be, it takes time and patience to make our mark in any profession. Till then it's the same story.

Dealing with past disappointments and moving ahead is one such difficult task to do. We know that disappointments from the past can linger and wreak havoc in your life if you let them. Becoming stuck in the past hinders you from making progress towards the future. It hampers your decision-making abilities, making you restless and incapable of moving ahead. It stops you from living the kind of life you want. Though it is very natural for one to feel sad and disappointed in the initial stage, it is better if one gets over it and moves ahead leaving their past behind. There may be situations where you are in a disappointing relationship or your attempted business plan failed to yield results. There are stages in life where you come across failures and disappointments, where you have failed to get the desired results. You should, try and forget that feeling as soon as possible and start making personal breakthroughs and start acknowledging them, so you can forget the past and propel yourself to a successful future.

Remember that everybody makes mistakes at some point in life and it is only human. Accept that you did your best even though it did not get you the desired outcome and quit blaming yourself over and over. There may be times, where you realize that the product that you have delivered was not up to the mark, and the client was not satisfied. That's okay, there is always scope for improvement. The first thing that you should do is to realize that and forgive yourself. If you made the wrong decisions, said or did something wrong to someone, or took unnecessary actions, you need to face that and forgive yourself for it.

The next thing that you can do is to appreciate what you have with you. In my case, it was my hard-working team that stood by me. It is their hard work and passion that helped us to get back to work with renewed energy and enthusiasm, and we kept doing our work and creating designs till we ended up constructing an award show set. Many sets have happened since and my team has always been there, putting their sweat and hard work into every project. The moment you start appreciating what you have and what you have managed to achieve, the less you will think about what you failed to get and what you may never have.

The main reason why people don't come out of their grief is that they forget to appreciate what they have, and they continue to rant about what they have lost. Learning to appreciate what you have will make you feel much happier. Learn to have a sense of appreciation for your team, your resources and even for your family members for standing by your side. They trust you and believe in what you do. Have a sense of gratitude towards them and you will never feel disappointed in your life.

Another thing that might lead you to disappointment is when you fail to come out of your comfort zone. If you keep sticking to your routine, and continue to stick around it, you will never grow. Unfortunately, this could be what is keeping you from making progress to a better future.

When you are willing to break your routine, you will realize that there is so much to love than getting hurt about the past. Accept the situation, take charge of it and be ready to start making changes. Be open to trying out new things. This change in your mind set will make you open to accepting more opportunities and will help you see things in a new light.

Now, there may be times, where in spite of working on all these changes, you might slip back into that uncomfortable zone where you feel bad for yourself. The best solution is to get busy in something that you have always loved to do. Even better, find something that you love the most in your job and go ahead working on it with full force. Get into it to such an extent that you don't have time to think of anything else. You will have two advantages of doing this. Firstly, you will come out of your gloominess. And secondly, you will be working on something that will again get you closer to achieve what you want.

Learn to create time for other things besides work - When you feel disappointed about something, your worst decision may be to bury yourself in your work in that you do not have time for anything else. This may work for a while in helping you forget. But it will do very little to improve the quality of life and to help you work towards a brighter future.

Next, look ahead to spend time with some positive minded friends and family members. Try meditating, reading an inspirational book, listening to some music that you like. These are all activities that can make a huge difference in helping you forget the past and will give you the energy you may need.

Remember, there is always a better tomorrow that you can look forward to. Forgiving yourself, having a sense of gratitude towards what you have, and working hard towards your next goal is the best antidote to past disappointments.

3. So what? Keep making mistakes

We all make mistakes in life. If we take up a challenging job, making mistakes is a part of the package. You are invited to make mistakes in your pursuit of completing a challenging job. In fact, more challenging the job is, you are more prone to making mistakes. It may be a job that you have been assigned to take care of, or it may be a personal challenge that you have never been into. Mistakes are a part of the learning process. Avoiding taking up challenges, in order to make less mistakes, is based on fear. It's okay to take up challenging jobs, even if it involves being wrong in places, because it gives you a chance to learn and grow, as the job progresses.

Making mistakes is not a problem, carrying them around in your heart is. Then there are some people, who enjoy pointing out others mistakes. They always have something to complain about, be it a bright sunny day or beautiful cloudy weather. And to make matters worse, such people have made it their habit. Such people make it a point to complain about everything, and they enjoy getting attention through it. Such chronic complainers are to be avoided at all costs. Keep away from such negative people, and don't let them disturb your piece of mind. The secret to growth is to avoid such people and continue taking up challenging jobs at the same time.

Then there are some simple goals that don't challenge you as much. They are very much within your capabilities and they don't challenge your capabilities as much. Let's call them easy-goals. Easy-goals are the ones which don't demand you to learn more, or do more. They are rather simple to achieve, and you don't feel uncomfortable while working on them. Such goals, are easy to check off the list, but are quite counterproductive in nature. Working on Easy-goals will never teach you anything new. Such goals, never let you discover your own potential. Neither do they involve making many mistakes. It's these goals that people like, as it shows, they are performing well in their jobs, usually keeping them in the good books of their bosses.

Another problem with pursuing such Easy-goals in the workplace is that, you might get tagged by your colleagues, and by your superiors with the kind of job you are good at. For example, I've seen a certain type of people, who are given similar jobs throughout their career, as they are only good at handling jobs of that level. These people are often termed as people trying to play the safe game. Better opportunities and challenges are generally handed over to those who are willing to take more risks and are willing to make mistakes on the way. Moreover, these safe gamers, don't have to worry about making mistakes during their whole career.

Let's look at the other clan of people who are ready to take risks, and to make mistakes in getting through tougher jobs. Let's call them Challengers. These people, are always ready to push the envelope, ready to go the extra mile, and ready to give some more. There might be a time, where these people might be getting nervous, would have their blood pressure racing upwards, but it does not deter these people from taking up challenging situations. These are the people who are known by their colleagues as the Better Ones.

These better ones, don't usually stick to a certain type of project. They are always on the move, ready to take risks, ready to take the plunge, and ready to get the results they want. They are the action takers in the game. Making mistakes is okay for them, and their core principle is to keep moving. They try to keep their energy and momentum focused on the challenging tasks that come their way and they are not bothered by anything that is keeping them away from their goal. Such people are also not deterred by what the other complainers have to say. They are just focused with getting the job done.

Now thinking upon it, whom do you feel is more likable to make more mistakes, a Safe-Gamer or a Challenger? The answer is obvious. While the Safe-Gamer is busy playing in a safe territory, he is too preoccupied with only applying knowledge and experience which already exist. It is the Challenger who rules the day.

Since making mistakes is also a part of the learning process, it becomes easy for the Challengers to avoid making mistakes as well. They continue to grow and learn as they move ahead. In fact, they being allowed to make more mistakes, usually turns them into people who don't err as much. Whereas, the Safe-Gamers are often seen as covering up on their mistakes as to keep their reputation clean. This is even more dangerous for the organization.

Another question to think about is, what if a mistake has been made? Whom do you think will admit more readily making a mistake and will be ready to amend it? Will it be a Safe-Gamer or a Challenger? Again, a challenger, will never hide their mistakes. Owning them up and working on rectifying it is the best thing a person can do for the growth of an organization. Be it the work place or the home, challengers are more capable of improving their performances and are definitely more capable in taking up difficult task than compared to the safe gamers.

If you want to be a challenger, be ready to take up challenges that need you to get out of your comfort zone. It might take a little more time in getting through tough jobs, you might even make more mistakes. These are the tasks which will help you grow and come out victorious in the end.

Finally, if you take up a challenge and at some point find yourself stuck in a situation, be ready to ask for help. Progress can never happen alone. The best way is to consult some experts on the way to success.

Be a game changer, this is how progress happens.

4. Does Goal Setting Bore you to Death?

Have you been struggling with goal setting? Do you really have a tough time when thinking about setting and accomplishing goals? For some people, just thinking of setting up a goal, or visualizing the outcome of a goal is a big problem. They cannot do it. Yet, if they try setting goals for themselves, they are setting them up for failure.

Now, if you belong to this certain group of people, who repeatedly fail at goal setting, there is no point in you setting up goals for yourselves. And if at all you do set goals and do not achieve it, it further puts your attitude in a downwards spiral and reduces your productivity and enthusiasm in everything you do.

There are some people who always live in a mindset of being a non-achiever of goals. They are clear about themselves about the fact that they can never achieve their goals. But the secret in emerging out of that mindset is to simply replace the word "Goal" with the word "Problem, aspiration, intention or anything else".

If you think that you can never reach a goal, try thinking it as a situation that you would want to handle by solving a certain problem. Now just by solving the problem, you are getting closer to achieving your goal. Everyone can solve problems, well most of us enjoy solving them. Now if we think of ourselves as problem solvers and continue solving them in a linear manner, it will surely make us move closer to what we want to achieve.

Let's say that you want to lose 10 kilos of weight and you make it as your goal. Now, you might try hard in the beginning and soon might tire yourself somewhere down the middle and give up on it. Now just the setting up of your goal, and not being able to lose 10 kilos will make you look like a poor goal setter. On the other hand if you think of it this way, and say to yourself, "My weight is a problem, I can solve the problem by losing 10 kilos," Now you have an agenda. This is your problem and you have to work on finding a solution of this by working on solving the problem.

This is the catch. All you have to do is to simply replace the word Goal Setting if you don't like it. Replacing it with words like problems, aspirations, tasks, etc. might get you back on your toes towards completing/solving it. The answer is to quit setting goals. It's just that you have to turn your statement into a new one by calling it something else.

If you want to do something like starting a new business, you can call it an intention. If you intend to do it, it will automatically motivate you to do something towards accomplishing it. Starting a new business can be an issue also. Now you have to deal with all the factors that have been a hindrance to solving this issue and the issues involved with your startup.

The issue may be lack of clients, lack of resources or product development. Now the way to solve these issues can be working on marketing or on working on research and development for your product. Once these issues are solved, you can move on to dealing with other problems and issues that come up.

Do you see the difference? It's only in the word. It's just a mental thing. Just by replacing the word, can help you think of it in a new manner and can keep you going. Change the word and it will change the actions, and if you will, the intentions towards it will also change. It's time to adopt new words and to get rid of the ones that are pulling you back.

The bottom line is this, if goal setting bores you to death, then stop setting goals. Give them new words. Call them intentions, issues, tasks, problems or anything else. Keep working on it till you identify what's preventing you from achieving what you want. Then simply take action and get over with it. Maybe, you will understand that they are the same thing. It's just a mental block. If you cannot be a goal setter, it's not a problem. You can be a problem solver, an issue solver, a doer, an achiever or anything else. It's just a word, and it's not boring every time.

❑

Chapter 10

Keep Going

That inner voice has both gentleness and clarity. So to get to authenticity, you really keep going down to the bone, to the honesty, and the inevitability of something.
–Meredith Monk

1. What about your backup? Reset your GPS

What do you do if the plan that you may have made for yourself doesn't work? Do you have an alternate plan? Most of the people keep following a certain path in their life without having a plan B. Even worse, many of them don't have a plan A in the first place. They just go about their life as it comes. Every time, a certain something falls into the lap of such a person, he simply accepts it or denies it and carries on. This is a case of absolute misery, which the people are not even aware of.

Many people leave their jobs without having any idea of what they are going to do to earn a living after they quit. They don't even have any idea of what they are going to do with their lives. It's not about the young adults or the new recruits who have just joined jobs and are trying out different avenues. Even older people in the middle of their respective careers don't know what to fall back on if they lose their jobs or have a sudden meltdown in their careers.

When you're in your twenties and thirties, you're still experimenting with different kinds of careers. That is when you're still deciding what you want to be and you do this by getting in and out of different jobs.

Though we know that people in their forties, have a fixed job, they have adjusted their lives based on their job profiles. They have their current standard of living based on their professions. People in their fifties are trying to get rid of their ongoing financial responsibilities, like their child's college education or marriage.

It does not matter on what stage of life we are, we should always be prepared of life taking a sudden twist or turn. This unexpected turn, if occurred in any stage of our career, especially in our senior years, can have some devastating effects. There won't be time to think of a Plan B time when we see our lives and careers come crumbling down.

Also in our senior years, we are already aware of our core strengths and weaknesses and have already given many years in learning the nuance of our profession. Any sudden twist in our career, will not give us time to reinvent ourselves and will lead to a very depressed state of mind. It is not only about the financial setback that might occur, the mental trauma is more painful.

Talking about the worldwide spread of the Covid-19 pandemic. We all know its devastating effect in our lives and it being a cause of major losses of many in their work front. From all the lives that were lost and all the families that had to learn how to go on without their loved ones, it has made us realize that we are not invincible. It has changed the landscape of this country in just about every way we can imagine. It also made us realize that, if we had come up with a Plan B as a country as well as in our personal lives, the scenario would have been different.

The best example of someone working on a Plan B is that in my own family. My brother, had to move out of his job as the sales head in one of the leading business organizations, due to the business downturn in Covid-19 pandemic. While the others in his team, struggled to look for jobs and to survive, my brother started to work on his own business idea that he had been thinking and trying to work upon since the past four years.

It was soon that my brother had his own successful business model running. He owns a flourishing online coaching business, where he mentors and coaches clients on how to market their businesses online. He also takes sessions on various topics like sales and guides his clients into developing their profiles. Now he is moving towards his next step as a business coach where he wants to mentor business heads to strive in their respective businesses effectively.

This is a perfect example of having a plan B in life. While he was in his job as the sales head in his previous organization, he worked on his goals of setting up a business model and was able to develop it into a full grown business as soon as he got his first opportunity.

My brother found his next goal, his next purpose in life, and was successfully able to turn his plan B into plan A.

There are a few leading influencers, who on the contrary feel that one should not have a plan B. They feel that, having a plan B as an option, gives you a chance of failure in plan A. It's more like burning your boats as you move forward. But, if we take the example of the Covid-19 pandemic, it was something that no one had ever thought of. It just happened and changed the lives of many. While this is an extreme example of change, keeping a plan B will always prepare you for what might happen. Working on a plan B is not about being afraid, or being worried, about plan A. It's about being more practical.

We all need to realize where we are and what is that we can do to reach the next level. It has to be specific to our desires. We need a GPS or a road map in our lives to do so.

It is time that we stop living our life in discontent. We all need to come out of our current situation and need to reclaim our lives. We need to take charge, take responsibility of our current situation and plan our next move much in advance.

No wonder that so many people are living lives of discontent? I repeat, it is not only that most people don't have a Plan B. Many of us don't even have a Plan A. They don't know where they're going or why they're here, so they drift aimlessly and call it living.

After all, having a plan B will serve you as your GPS to take you to the next level of success.

2. The Three 'W's of inspiration

Do you know the three elements that are necessary for every goal, every desire to manifest. The conceptualization of these elements are of utmost importance if you want to achieve something.

We can call them the three W's. With even one W missing, you won't be able to achieve anything that you have desired.

The first W is of 'What'. If you don't have a clear vision of what you want to achieve, the whole concept of goal setting becomes a sham. For this you must have a clear vision of 'what' you want. It's like creating a vision board for yourself. And when I say clear vision it includes having some photos, some graphics or some designs. In fact it is even better to have it in front of you so that you come across it many times in a day. The more you see your vision board during your daily routine, more are the chances of you working towards achieving your goals.

Then comes the second W which we have already spoken about many times in this book. It's that of having a 'Why'. Having a solid reason and a sound motive to achieve the goal is even more important than 'What' you want to achieve. It is this 'Why' that gives you fuel to keep moving ahead towards your 'What'.

This 'why' is a clear reason for the passion and energy that drives every person to move towards his goal? It gives the person energy to keep going and to face all kinds of adversities that comes in ones way in pursuit of their goals.

"Why" for me has often been the reason I have strived towards my family goals. A few years back, I and my wife often spent time discussing about why we needed a new apartment. This new apartment that we wanted was not just about buying one, because we needed extra space. Of course, the extra space was always welcome. It was also about trying to give our parents and daughter better amenities and surroundings. This common 'why' was enough for getting me and my wife motivated towards achieving the goal. Although it did take us a couple of years, we were soon able to purchase a bigger and a better apartment.

So you should think of a clear 'why'. Spend some time with yourself and come up with a solid concrete 'why' that will help you move forward. If you work as a team or you lead the organization, having a common 'why' gives fuel to your collective goal. Never underestimate the power of having a clear and precise 'why' in your journey towards your goals.

Once you have worked upon the 'what' and 'why' the next step is to work upon the 'when'. Attaching a timeline to your goal is so very important. As I had stated earlier, a goal without a timeline, is a wish. What is the use of just wishing and not achieving something?

The next step is to create a clear outline of how do you intend to achieve your goal. You should have a plan for action, to keep you going in the right direction. If you know what to do, and are also emotionally charged about it, but you don't have a plan to pursue, what is the use of all this? Plan, prepare and act. As simple as that. Do this and you are better off than so many other people in the world.

Now that you know the way to proceed, are you ready to take the plunge? If you think you are all set to achieve your goals, please pause for a moment. Yes, wait for a while. There is still something that you should know. It's the secret method of enhancing ones discipline.

The secret is about dividing your time efficiently. Working on this will enhance your progress tremendously.

The secret is this, when you plan… Just Plan. Don't execute.

When you execute, just do it. Just take action. Don't keep planning.

Well, you can divide your time accordingly. It's better to simplify your goals into achievable bits that you can work upon on a daily basis. Plan on how you will do it and get going. Don't stop, and don't 'Over plan'.

Once you have this in mind, you just need to apply it in every aspect of your life. Daily. The next time you have to do your task, start it precisely at whatever time you have planned for working on it. Do it as if it was the most important meeting or conversation of your life. Because it is. Why? All big things are made up of small things. And these small things will only be done if... you do them.

Discipline is the word. Any task that is done on a regular basis, even little by little, turns into a habit. This habit takes about a month to get installed in your system. Let's say, you start lifting weights daily, the first day might be more difficult but don't worry. It will get easier. Repeat it every day at the same time. Slowly, you will gain strength to add more weights to your workout and you will definitely enjoy your exercise more. Once, this habit is formed, you will do it with no effort at all. The reward of gaining more strength and muscle, and have a fitter body will be a well-deserved award for the new habit that you have installed.

Now, an extra tip, to help you keep on track, while you install new habits into your system. In this weight lifting analogy, best results are achieved if you keep track of the amount of weight, number of exercises, and repetitions etc. by noting it down on a regular basis. This helps you keep track of your small achievements. These achievements, slowly compound into beautiful, tangible results. Such small results will be your reference points in your journey towards your success.

3. The Important Pessimist

One thing that we all now know is that, in our quest to reach the destination, is that there should be a lot of joy in the journey. If we do not enjoy the journey, there is no point in reaching your destination.

There is another group of people, who worry a lot on their journey. They are the typical, so called negative thinkers. In general, we are often told by the experts to avoid all type of negative people. They are said to bring negative thinking into the task in hand and this in turn slows down the growth process. These thinkers have a constant worrying habit which inhibits growth and progress.

But worrying in all is also a type of thinking. It is based on bad thoughts created from one conceptual situation. It is not about negative thinking or about being a pessimist, there is a good side to it. Having a negative thinker in the group has a few benefits. It gives us an opportunity to see things from the other side. They help us in showing us the situation in a different perspective. I am not disparaging the good side of a positive attitude and optimism.

Negative people are the ones who are always aware of the possible problem. They often think of an outcome which in general is overlooked by an optimist. Also, these people prevent a person to become over confident in their endeavour. A pessimist is also a good analyst, who if takes care of his worrying problem, can spot leakages in the process.

They are also similar to the positive thinker in certain ways. It is that they both are good at imagining outcomes. The only difference is in the direction of the outcome. The only corollary here is that a negative thinker does not have to plan for a negative thing to happen while an optimist has to prepare to avoid all possible downfalls.

Then there is a negative thinker who is thinking ahead of the situation. He remains extra careful by planning his activities around the problem and making sure that the problem does not happen in the first place.

They are also realistic in their approach. While the optimist might be a little extravagant in his approach, the negative thinker will have practical and time bound solution to the problems. This happens much early before the outcome changes towards the worse.

Being specific in our thoughts and careful planning is the best we can do to avoid hurdles. This planning is the best we can do to avoid any sort of negative outcome. If at all, you tend to become dreamy or get over ambitious, remind yourself of the negative thinker friend that you have, and the way he will deal with it.

At times, negative thoughts end with positive outcomes. They help us reach our goals, the real and practical way.

A pessimist can be your saviour, the one who shows you what no optimist can.

4. Finally, a total commitment to your goals

To commit to a goal means making a promise to ourselves and to others. It is a serious vow that we are driven to accomplish something worthwhile. It means that once you commit to something, you are ready to give 100% of what it needs and are not holding back anything. It also means that you are ready to take the responsibility of the ups and downs and are ready to fight for it whatever it takes.

This is what we need to do with our goals. There should be lifetime commitments and not just shallow promises. It's these lifetime commitments that drive us and give us the energy to keep going. In many ways we can compare the goals to that of maintaining a relationship with your spouse. Striving towards your goals, as well as marriage demands total commitment on your part.

In a marriage, we need to commit to our spouses. Without any hatred and resentment, without any competition, it's all about building and maintaining a healthy relationship. It's about nurturing the relationship on an everyday consistent basis.

In goals also, we need to commit to its outcome. Without any resentment or selfishness, we need to give our time to move on the path to achieving the desired goal. Here also, we need to give all it needs without holding anything back.

Another common factor that goals and marriages have in common is that they both should be congruent to our core values. All successful marriages rely on values that spouses respect in a mutual way.

Keeping faith in achieving our goal, giving it total time and dedication, supporting that goal is just like what we do in marriages. If you are selfish and unsupportive towards your spouse, and are not ready to give the relationship the time and attention it needs, it's bound to fail. Similar results happen if goals are treated in this way.

Both, committing to a goal and to commit in a relationship, demands a lot of learning as well. There will be times when your faith will be tested. There will be moments in a relationship, as well as in getting to your goal, that you will feel that nothing worthwhile is happening. At times, getting to your goal, or a relationship might feel boring. But these are testing times. These are the times where you need to reset your compass, and should be ready to put in some extra care and effort to keep things going in the right direction. But, anything that you put should not be forced upon, neither towards a goal or in a relationship.

Not to forget, being a failure in a goal, or in a relationship also involves a lot of guilt and resentment. If you are not ready to give it all that it needs, it's simply not worth it. It's good to keep working and nurturing your goal and your relationship, than to fret and feel guilty about the whole thing.

Say, you still feel you are not getting what you want. But if you have given everything it needs, and it still doesn't work out in a good way, at least you won't end up ridden with guilt. That itself is a sort of win on your part. The feeling, that at least you tried your best, will give you the courage to brush things off and will give you the courage to keep moving ahead. But not trying, or not committing, is not an option.

Commitment means giving both our goals and our relationships, the undivided attention they need. In so many cases, people make loose promises, without being serious, and end up in a mess. That is why all such promises and commitments should be made and taken seriously. Commitment is the word to be followed. So make real promises, give it all it needs, and just commit.

❑

Chapter 11

Fun & Gratitude

"Gratitude is a powerful catalyst for happiness. It's the spark that lights a fire of joy in your soul."

– Amy Collette

1. What does Fun cost? Where is it?

Now that we have discussed so much about the topic of goal setting, we need to talk about the time needed to get things moving. All said and done, the moment we get ourselves in motion, we need to remind us of the most important element of our journey. It's to have fun.

Now what is fun, you may ask. Fun is simply where you begin to enjoy every part of your goal setting process. It's a state of mind where you reach a level of mental peace, however stressful your job at hand may be.

The best way to accomplish our task is to get totally involved and engrossed in it. Author Mihaly Csikszentmilhayi, in his famous bestseller Flow, has explained this state of mind in great detail. It is this state that everyone of us should strive to attain. It is a meditative state, where one gets so much engrossed in his task, that he loses track of space and time and finds himself enjoying every bit of the task. This usually takes the doer onto the next level of consciousness and the doer is transcended to a state of joy and bliss.

A similar concept has been described in the Bhagwad Geeta in the chapters of Karma Yoga. The Bhagwad Geeta explains the karma yogi to be a person with a similar state of consciousness explained above. The involvement of the doer, in the task that he is doing, increases to such a level, that the doer is not bothered about the result of the task. He simply keeps on doing his bit, giving his best in every moment, and does not worry about the end result of the task.

This state of super-consciousness is the fun we are talking about. It is the state where even the final outcome of the task does not matter anymore. What matters is the doer's complete involvement in the task that he is doing.

This happy zone is the one where we have no connection with the outer word, we are not distracted by anything, and we continue to do our job with 100% effort and involvement. In this zone, even the amount of time spent on doing the job does not matter and many times the doer himself gets surprised when he notices the amount of time that has passed without him being aware of it.

When any task, either easy, or difficult, small or big, is done in such a manner, the doer finds himself doing every bit of the given task with total involvement and finds himself enjoying every part of it.

Have you ever noticed the feeling when you do such a task? For me, it happens, during the time I am doing my set designs. Picking up a piece of paper to draw my set designs is the time where I'm transported to another level. It is just the piece of paper and my drawing pen. Nothing else matters beyond this, till I am able to create a unique set design that is congruent to my thought process. It goes on till I am contended with my design.

We as doer can sit and decide the time of the day where we can do such work without getting bothered by any external distractions. Some people prefer to work early in the morning. The best example of a morning person is the author Robin

Sharma, who prefers working early in the morning, and has numerous examples of this in his bestselling book, The 5 A.M. club. So much so that he silently persuades everyone to wake up early and to rule the world. Then, on the other side are the night people, who find themselves working at their best late during the night. Most of them feel that it's best to work distraction free when the world sleeps. They feel that they can give their best at that time to make their dreams come true, when the others are busy dreaming.

Being a night person or a morning person is just a matter of choice. What matters here is to be in that zone where you simply enjoy doing your work. This is the zone where we all intend to be while working on our tasks.

Now is the time for you to choose the time of the day, get rid of all the distractions, and start having fun.

Now we come to the second part of having fun. If asked to a number of adults, of what their idea of having fun is, many of them might start giving each other a weird look. They might think that the idea of fun is only meant for kids. Having fun in adult life is only about having an active social life, with lots of parties, and lots of drinking alcohol and dancing through the night.

This idea of fun is a very subjective one and it changes from person to person. Apart from this, these people cannot relate to any other idea of having fun. The rest of the things that they do, start to bore them. These people, either feel that they should be working, which is boring, or they should be partying, and that is what they look forward to every weekend. Most people in the corporate world wait for Friday nights to drown themselves in alcohol and other modes of addiction to get back to their senses on Monday morning, looking forward towards another Friday night.

Is this fun? Or is kids playing games, running around is fun?

If it is kids, who have fun, playing games with each other, you might think that you have crossed that age, and you have nothing of that sort of thing left in your life to look forward to.

There must be an easier and a simpler answer to this. Don't we deserve a better answer to the question of having fun?

To have fun is a combination of everything you do, till the time it does not feel tedious. It can be working and staying in that transcended zone of mental consciousness. It can even be getting totally involved in playing a game or a sport. You can even join the kids in the game and be a part of their role play to have fun. Even partying and boozing and dancing the whole night is a good idea of fun.

It all works relatively and is based on your mindset. It's just that you have to be ready to have fun in everything you do. Just the willingness to be fully involved in everything is the core idea of having fun. This is the trick and this is the best technique.

Fun is something that is done with your heart in it. At times even the result does not matter to you. It is purely and simply something that you want to do with full involvement. Anything that brings a warm smile on your face and a sense of satisfaction, of doing something good can be termed as having fun.

Now there is no excuse for us of not having time or resources to have fun. It's just like play, the outcome does not matter. The focus and involvement is only what is needed to get you your dose of fun.

Only thing that we have to take care of is that what we do should not have a bad consequence on ourselves as well as others. This is the price we have to pay for not knowing when we have crossed the line of fun. If done wholeheartedly, and with full consciousness, we are able to know the difference between good and bad fun. Once this is taken care of, we are ready to enter the fun zone and enjoy every bit of life as it comes.

Nothing is more fulfilling than getting into a state where you can fill yourself with emotional satisfaction while enjoying every bit of your life's journey.

2. What all Successful People never Forget to do!

I'm sure if you have reached this section, you have been longing to be successful in whatever you have been doing. We all want to be successful. We all want change to happen in our worlds, and that too for the better. It may not be a very dramatic change on the outside, but a subtle shift on the inside which will lead you to what you want. Now everyone has a different definition of success. Everyone sees and evaluates it differently. But there is one thing in common in all successful people. They simply don't give up. When the course is hard, they try harder. They simply never give up.

There is no such thing as No Success. These people simply don't have this option. They may try a different approach of what they are trying, but successful people don't keep success with other options. They consider it as the only option. It's simple, Quitting is not an option.

They know that if obstacles do arise, the best way is the way forward. In the words of Zig Ziglar, "You might have to change direction, but do not change the decision to be there."

Success is all about having fun and enjoying what you are doing. You may decide to try your hand at soccer. You may get enough attention from your friends and family. You may get enough cheer from your fans on the field. You might even have some excellent people giving you tips. You might even end up being a part of a state soccer team and might even shoot a goal in a match. But the real success is not in shooting a goal. The success happens between you deciding to play soccer, and you shooting the goal. It happens during those in between times when no one is watching. It happens when no one but you cares about it. This is the fun part, and you need to learn to enjoy this. Doing whatever it takes to reach that point where you have shot the goal is the journey to success and you need to enjoy the ups and downs of it.

Also you might have had previous successes, which you thought were very hard to achieve but you had finally made it.

There must have been times where you must have thought of giving up, but you continued doing it till it became second nature. There might have been times where some tasks may have been very difficult, but with continuous practice and persistence, you decided to continue and are now an expert in it.

Let me tell you about a friend Sunil's incident about overcoming fear. The first time Sunil held the steering wheel of his new car, he did not know driving. Abhay, who himself was an experienced driver, took to the passenger seat to assist him to drive. They stood on an empty straight road, some two hundred meters long that turned right around the corner and ended in a dead end. Me and my other friends stood nearby watching Sunil learn his first driving lesson.

As Sunil shifted his car in gear and released his foot from the clutch, the car took a jerk and ran, heading towards the end of the road. Though the car was in first gear, he nervously continued accelerating, instead of pulling the brakes. Every one of us, who saw the car shoot and gain speed had the scare of our life. Within seconds, the road would have ended and either Sunil could have steered right, or would have ended in a wall.

It was then that Abhay, jumped from the passenger's seat and stuck his leg and pressed hard onto the brake pedal. The car screeched to a halt. Sunil jumped out of the car sweating and shivering. He scowled and vowed never to touch the steering wheel again.

It's been a few months to this story and Sunil has now become an excellent car driver, and can shift gears, accelerate and brake with ease. So much so, that he enjoys driving. It's simple, giving up driving, just because you have had a scary experience, is simply not worth it.

This may be a simple example, but it is relevant to all the things we do. Anything new that we try to learn may be as difficult in the beginning. The hardest thing to do is to stay on the course, and to never give up.

3. Do we now have the Tips to Success?

When looking for success in any field, it always helps to identify and emulate the methods of other successful people. Speaking to them and understanding their methods will always give you the factors you need to accomplish your goals. Here we will discuss a few such factors that can help you to excel in your journey to success.

- Whatever be your field of endeavor, it always pays to be the best in your field. It is the best who always get the best, and the average who always get the average. To work with the mediocre mindset will always give you mediocre results.
- If we look at any world class player, we should notice the amount of sweat and hard work he has put in to be there. Sachin Tendulkar, spent endless hours in the nets practicing his batting skill, even at odd hours. It's his belief and hard work that got him to the place he deserved. It is said that for any business to excel, it needs to be given 1000 days of hard work and relentless effort. It is only after this consistent effort do the results begin to show. Performance of all world class cricket players like M.S Dhoni, Virat Kohli , are all a result of the endless hours that they have spent practicing on improving their skills in the game. On a personal front, Author Robin Sharma suggests giving 10,000 hours of practice of any skill to get into the zone of mastery. It is this practice, which will make you reach for the skies, and make you an expert in any field.

- To be at the top of the game also needs you to believe in your potential. No one will believe in you more than yourself. If you believe that you are awesome, then you are. Thinking highly about yourself, builds a high self-esteem, which shows in your work. A word of caution here is that we should learn to control our ego. Too much of self-esteem, slowly manifests into self-pride, which makes one egoistic and selfish. To believe in oneself, and not being egoistic about it is what we should take care of. To be humble, and to serve others, is the true mark of the master. One such example is that of Ratan Tata, owner and chairperson of the Tata Group of Industries. His loving, caring and philanthropic attitude, makes him a true leader.
- Being an expert in your field of endeavor, give you more confidence to speak about your field. The better speaker you are, it gives you more control, as you become good at communicating to others of what you have to offer to others which are better than your competitors. To learn to speak with confidence, is one of the best things that you can do for the people whom you serve as well as work for. While you speak with confidence, you also must become more teachable and coachable and open to learn more. The more you learn, the more you will hear yourself sounding like an expert at what you are talking about.
- My mother's favorite words for anything good that happens in our life is that it's "God's Grace". We often use these word, connecting them to every small incident

that occurs in our family. Every little victory, according to my mother is due to "God's grace", and we never forget acknowledging this fact. Even writing this book for you to read is "God's Grace". You being able to hold this book and read these words is again "God's Grace". It can be anyone, maybe God, your Parents, friends, children or well-wishers. Being grateful to them for everything you have is the most important tip in ones journey to success. Always be grateful to the people around you, and let the world know that you acknowledge them. The least you can do is to live with this fact, and help other people also grow through your love and care.

4. Shouldn't we be enjoying the Journey?

Goals are a vital component of self-development and allows us to live a much more fulfilling life. It is our goals that drive and motivate us to move ahead. That is why we set goals.

But there are some goals which do not have an end. For example, being a good husband, a good wife, or a good parent. Being a loving and a caring husband can be a goal but it does not have an end. It is an ongoing journey. It is like putting your money in your investment account. To help it grow, it needs time and patience, along with continuous and regular deposits. Its only when invested on a regular basis will it give you the benefits of compounding.

Its only when we continue working on being a better parent or a husband, do we enjoy the love and care of our family, and keep cherishing it for a long time. If you were a loving parent today but you fail to be one tomorrow; you are no longer a loving parent.

Every goal that is relative to us has the same thought process behind it. If we keep focusing on the destination and don't concentrate on the process and the journey, it does us more harm than good.

We become fixated on the goal, the outcome, and the results. This mind set is unhealthy. It's not in the destination that we should be focusing on. Instead, it always pays more to focus on the journey.

Imagine a scene where, on a cloudy morning you decide to explore the hillside with your friends. Suppose, you and your friends, Mohit and Anuj are having a good time walking towards a broken pathway when suddenly Mohit comes up with an idea. When you reach the bottom of the hill, Mohit suggests that we climb to the top to enjoy breathtaking views of the other side.

While Mohit, who is on the fitter side is enthusiastic to get to the top, there seems to be a problem with Anuj, who is a bit on the heavier side. He is not very enthusiastic to climb, but at the same time wants to enjoy the beautiful view as well. He does not want to miss the scenery.

In the beginning, your ascent seems to be a smooth climb. Soon, the terrain turns a little rough, with loose gravel sometimes, sliding from under the feet as you step forward. It seems that you all have misjudged the condition of the terrain a bit. A few minutes up the hill and we hear Anuj's voice.

"Are we there yet?"

"How long until we get there?"

The climb is not easy for Anuj. At the same time he does not want to feel left out. Being a bit on the heavier side, he starts to breathe heavily. Sweating profusely he tries to keep up the pace with the other two friends. He might be a little uncomfortable, but he also wants to reach the top and enjoy the view.

To make matters worse, it starts to drizzle. This slow drizzle, irritates Anuj even more. This climb becomes more painful, when the path slowly starts to become muddy and slippery.

Now Anuj, on the verge of losing his patience, tries to speed himself up a bit. He seems to be lagging behind, while trying to keep his foot strongly on the ground, so that he doesn't slip.

His mind keeps coming up with statements like these:

"To hell with the climb"

"I hope it doesn't start to rain heavily"

"I really want to get back down, why is everyone walking so fast?"

Mohit, on the other hand, has a different approach. He's equally excited about reaching the top and see the beautiful view of the valley. Yet, his attitude is different. He looks at the scenery around him, marvels at the plants and foliage around him. He enjoys the light splatter of rain on his shoulders and feels the light breeze on his face as he continues climbing up the hill. . He loves feeling the grass on his feet and loves hopping over the slippery puddles that come his way. And, he takes an approach of appreciating the journey itself. He's eager to reach the top but he finds the journey itself quite pleasurable too.

Finally you all manage to reach the top, and you get to see the amazing, breathtaking view of the beautiful valley with the other hills around it.

Suppose you reach there and realize that the view of the valley has been blocked by the clouds and you are not able to see anything. Also it has started to rain a bit heavily and you have to get back down before the rain intensifies any further. Anuj would be quite upset with this. After so much trouble, he would feel that the long and annoying journey was all for nothing. He has gotten nothing out of the journey. While Mohit will also be a bit upset with this, maybe as much as Anuj is, but at least he enjoyed the journey. His day is not completely ruined and he's still got an opportunity to enjoy his trek on his way up and down.

Too many times, we make the same mistake as what Anuj made in the above example.

Whatever the goal is, we often concentrate only on the outcome of it. Of course, the end result is important, but to enjoy the process will make you happier. Also, having a clear end in mind will keep you focused in that specific direction, but if you keep just the end in mind, and skip the beauty of the process, you have missed a lot of experience that comes your way.

Your goal can be anything as simple as helping your child work on his school project. Or it can be cracking the new deal with the client. It can be anything that's personal or professional. The more we stay aware of enjoying the process, the more of a fun activity it becomes. Don't treat your goals like a regular chore with no enthusiasm or energy involved. Remember, the journey is often more important than the destination.

The best we can do is to firstly, plan and decide on the goal, then create a plan and focus on completing the goal in time.

Try looking at life without losing focus on the larger things, while enjoying the smaller bits of it at the same time. Do this as often as you can, and you are ready to enjoy life to the fullest.

❑